P9-CMQ-933

DATE DUE

MAR 2 2			
MAY 07 199			
OCT 02 199			
OCT 29 1997			
GAYLORD			PRINTED IN U.S.A.

THE
HANK AARON
STORY

As a quiet, hard-working boy of twelve, Henry
"Hank" Aaron had only one pastime—baseball. A topnotch sandlotter, he also played
softball and football at grammar and high
school. At eighteen, he was playing in the
tough Negro League, and his over .400 batting
average attracted major league scouts. He was
signed by the Braves, and has since been
making baseball history. Considered "one of
the greatest natural hitters of all time," he
was voted the Most Valuable Player in 1957
and has already won several batting titles,
including his second RBI title in 1960.

Books by Milton J. Shapiro

THE SAL MAGLIE STORY

JACKIE ROBINSON OF THE BROOKLYN DODGERS

THE WARREN SPAHN STORY

THE ROY CAMPANELLA STORY

THE PHIL RIZZUTO STORY

THE MEL OTT STORY

THE WILLIE MAYS STORY

THE GIL HODGES STORY

THE HANK AARON STORY

A BEGINNER'S BOOK OF SPORTING GUNS AND HUNTING

MICKEY MANTLE: YANKEE SLUGGER

THE
HANK AARON
STORY

B 43

By *Milton J. Shapiro*

ILLUSTRATED WITH PHOTOGRAPHS

JULIAN MESSNER, INC.   ·   NEW YORK

BLAIRSVILLE SENIOR HIGH SCHOOL
BLAIRSVILLE, PENNA.

Published by Julian Messner, Inc.
8 West 40 Street, New York 18

Published simultaneously in Canada
by The Copp Clark Publishing Co. Limited

© Copyright 1961 by Milton J. Shapiro

Third printing, 1962

Photographs used with the permission of Wide World Photos

Printed in the United States of America

Library of Congress Catalog Card No. 61-6371

*With grateful acknowledgment
to Bill Carr for his help in the
preparation of this book*

1...

It was one of those warm, excessively humid days that come at times to the city of Mobile in early April. The afternoon sun hung dull yellow, and over the fields and the dirt roads the pink dust of Alabama's red clay earth hung like a pall. Down South Wilkerson Street, in the Toulminville section of the city, a squat old ice truck lumbered tiredly, water dripping a dark trail from its lowered tailgate. The truck stopped in front of a small shack of peeling tan clapboard and instantly was surrounded by a swarm of squealing children.

"Piece of ice! Piece of ice!" they chorused to the heavy man who lowered himself from the truck's cab and walked toward them. He grunted and scowled at the children, but to each he gave a small piece of dripping ice which they grabbed quickly and sucked at noisily. Then the man turned to a short, wiry boy of perhaps eleven who had climbed down from the other side of the cab and stood waiting quietly.

"Well Henry," the man said, "sure you can handle it okay? I don't want your Ma jumpin' on me if you hurt yourself, hear? This ice ain't feathers, y'know."

The boy nodded, lips set. "I'm a lot stronger than I look. Besides, you promised, remember?"

The man sighed, took a handkerchief from the back pocket of his trousers and mopped his face. "Hottest April I recollect, even for Mobile," he said, giving himself a moment more to think it over. Then he shrugged. "Okay Henry. I'll give you a chance. But mind now, if you get hurt it's your own fault, hear?" With that he boosted himself, grunting, onto the truck's rear platform and set about cutting a chunk of ice from a huge, burlap-covered cake. First, after removing the burlap, he scribed the piece to be cut with the point of his ice tongs, then chopped away at the scribed line with a sharp-pointed pick until the piece broke free. He kicked it to the edge of the platform, jumped to the ground, swung the ice cake off the truck with the tongs and handed the grips to the boy. "It's all yourn," he said.

The boy clutched at the iron tongs nervously; as he took them the weight of the ice jerked him forward. But he straightened grimly, and tugging the ice at his side, fingers aching from the tong handles, he staggered up the short walk of the clapboard house, banged on the door with his elbow. Agonizing moments later a woman opened it, blinked at him, then stared, openmouthed. "Henry Aaron," she gasped. "What you doin' carrying that ice?"

His shoulders were on fire. His arms seemed to be pulling out of their sockets. "You ordered ice, didn't you?" he said, trying to be brave and casual. He hoped

10

she would let him in quickly before he dropped the ice.

She seemed to recognize his plight. "Come on in here boy," she said, standing aside so he could pass by her in the narrow doorway. She followed him as he staggered through a dark hallway to a kitchen in the rear of the house. She helped him lift the ice into its compartment in the ancient icebox, all the while clucking her tongue and chattering at him in her amazement at finding him working at such a task. When they were finished she gave him a glass of water from the tap. While he gulped greedily she reached for her purse. "How come you haulin' ice like you was a grown man, Henry?" she said, putting some coins in his hand. "I heard your Pa was doin' all right workin' for that shipbuilding company."

Henry put down the glass, wiped his lips with his forearm. "Oh he is. But I gotta make my own money for goin' to the ball game."

"Ball game?" she repeated. "You breakin' your back to make money for seein' a little old ball game?"

"It ain't just any game," he said. "The Dodgers are playing the Red Sox Saturday. It's a big league exhibition game."

She looked at him blankly, and he shook his head. "I gotta go now," he said. "I can only work two hours after school. Then I gotta get home." He began to walk down the hall.

"Wait a minute," she called after him. He returned and she went to her purse again. Hesitantly, she re-

11

moved another coin. She clutched it in her fingers a moment, then put it quickly in Henry's hand. He stared at it, then up at her. She smiled. "Who all'd you say was playin' Saturday?"

He grinned. "Dodgers and Red Sox." He turned again and raced for the door. "Thanks a lot!" he cried over his shoulder. She stood in the kitchen for a moment, gazing absently down the gloom of the hallway toward the door to the street. Then, singing quietly to herself, she went back to work.

In the street, Henry climbed back into the truck and gave the iceman his money. "She gave me a tip," he said. "Look. A nickel!"

"Good. Good," the iceman said. "But I was watching you. You were straining yourself. You sure you want to keep helping?"

"I wasn't straining!" he retorted hotly. "I told you I was strong. Now come on, let's get goin' to the next stop."

The iceman shrugged. If the boy wanted to knock himself out for tip money, why should he worry? He started the truck rolling again down South Wilkerson Street.

It was near four o'clock when the ice truck turned into Edwards Street and rolled to a stop before the house numbered 2010. It was a frame house of weathered gray with a sagging porch that hung across the front and along one side. Henry bounced down from the cab and ran up the short flight of wooden steps. He turned for a moment at the door, called to the ice-

12

man—"Same time tomorrow!"—then went inside. Only when the door at last closed behind him did he allow the weariness to take hold of his body. It washed over him like a wave, sent him exhausted, in a heap, to a sofa in the front parlor.

The next afternoon, when classes were over at Toulminville Grammar School, Henry again climbed aboard the ice truck, returning home hours later arms weary and back aching—but with coins jingling in his pocket for balm.

The next day was Saturday. He rose early, dressed and went to the kitchen. His mother was already there, stirring cereal in a big iron pot on the stove. Estella Aaron was a cheerful woman, round and smiling-eyed. She tasted a spoonful of the cereal, added a shake of salt, then poured a bowlful and put it on the kitchen table in front of her son. "You goin' to that baseball game today?" she asked, seating herself at the table with a cup of coffee.

Henry nodded, spooning cereal rapidly into his mouth.

"Then what are you hurryin' like that for? The game don't start till one o'clock and it ain't near nine yet."

"Got a coupla lawns to mow this morning."

She snorted. "Boy, how come all of a sudden you so interested in baseball? I ain't never seen you work so hard before. You work like that later on and you might make yourself a lot of money when you're a man."

"Oh don't worry about me. I'm gonna make plenty of money when I get big."

13

"You are? Doin' what?"

He stopped eating for a moment. "I don't know." He seemed surprised, as though no one had ever asked him the question before and he had never had to think of it. He shrugged. "Doin' something, I guess."

She chuckled. "Now that's reassurin'."

"Well I haven't figured it out yet, that's all. Maybe if the war's over when I grow up I'll go to college or something." He pushed back his chair. "Gotta run," he said, and dashed from the house.

He was seated, several hours later, in the wooden bleacher section of Hartwell Field, gazing downward with numbing awe at the uniformed men on the playing area. In that spring of 1945, in the waning days of the Second World War, Henry was seeing a diluted version of big league baseball. The Brooklyn Dodgers and the Boston Red Sox, as did all other teams in organized baseball, fielded patchwork clubs while the stars were serving in the Armed Forces. Henry was nonetheless impressed with such as pitcher Tex Hughson and infielder Bobby Doerr of the Red Sox, and with such Dodgers as catcher Mickey Owen, infielders Eddie Stanky and Eddie Miksis, outfielder Luis Olmo, and the Brooklyn club's famous, fiery manager, Leo Durocher.

For hours, while the teams loafed through their practice sessions, and then played spiritedly through a Dodger victory, Henry sat alone and quiet on his wooden bench, his eyes never leaving the field. It was his first visit to Hartwell Field, his first view of a major league ball game. He went away profoundly moved. For the next two weeks, as other major league teams moved through Mobile on their way north for opening day of the regular season, Henry spent his spare money and time at Hartwell Field watching the exhibition games. During the summer months he toiled and wracked his body on the ice truck and behind the lawn mowers, earning more money to see more baseball, minor league baseball played by the Mobile club of the Southern Association.

Still, for all his avid interest in baseball, it was only a spectator sport for Henry Aaron. At Toulminville Grammar School he played softball, the school had no baseball team, and his participation in sandlot baseball was indifferent. When his friends or classmates would choose up sides for a pick-up game Henry would often shrug them off. "Rather go over to Hartwell Field and see a real game," was his stock answer, and he would spend his last, hard-earned cent for an admission ticket.

He continued his hard work on the ice truck and with the lawn mower, and in the spring of 1946 the Dodgers were back in Mobile, on their way north once again in the waning weeks of spring training. These Dodgers were different. They were the first of the post-war Dodgers, the team that revolutionized baseball. On that squad was Jackie Robinson, organized baseball's first Negro, destined later that year to be sent to their Montreal farm team.

In the bleachers at Hartwell Field that spring, stirred

15

by something he was yet too young to recognize, Henry Aaron sat quietly and watched Jackie Robinson play brilliantly with a major league ball club. He returned to his home on Edwards Street that evening an older and more serious-minded boy.

At the dinner table he ate in thoughtful silence.

"Something wrong with you boy?" his father asked. "How come you ain't clackin' around like a crow like you usually do when we eatin'?"

"He was out at Hartwell Field today," said Henry's older brother Herbert, chuckling. "Bet he ate too many hot dogs. Didn't you, Henry?"

"Leave the boy be," said Estella Aaron, leaving the stove to sit at the table. "Just 'cause the boy ain't sitting there making noise like the rest of you is no reason to be pickin' on him."

"I ain't sick or nothing," Henry said. He put down his fork. "I just been thinking, that's all. And you know what I been thinking?" He waited a moment, looking around the table before continuing. "I decided that when I grow up I'm gonna be a baseball player."

The table was silent. Then his mother, eyes wide in astonishment, clucked her tongue softly. She was about to say something teasing to him, but she saw the serious look on his face and changed her mind. Instead she said simply, "Henry, pass down them mashed potatoes!"

2 . . .

For all the noise coming from the sidelines the action
on the field might have been a major league ball game
instead of a teen-age sandlot contest. The youngsters
of Mobile took their baseball as seriously as anybody.
The Mobile City Recreation League was, in a modest
way, their own kind of advanced Little League, and
to the youngsters of the Toulminville area the Mobile
Bears, at bat now against their arch rivals, the Tigers,
were the best, most exciting team in the league.

Especially since Henry Aaron came to play for them.
He stood there at the plate now, a tall, lean fellow of
sixteen, relaxed, bat half-cocked lazily over his shoulder, apparently quite oblivious to the cheers and en-
treaties of the Bears' partisans in the crowd. It was
only the fourth inning of the game, the Bears trailing
2-0, but the fans were confident that Henry would
start a rally soon.

"He made out last time," a fan said to a neighbor,
"and there ain't many pitchers around can get ol'
Henry out two times in a row."

At the plate Henry let a pitch go by for a ball; an-

17

other for a strike. He barely moved a muscle as he stood there waiting, his eyelids fairly drooping. His coach on the Central High School softball team had once remarked that Henry seemed to be half asleep when he batted—until the pitch came that he wanted.

It came now—and Henry uncoiled like a striking snake. He met the ball squarely and sent it on a blurred line to left center field. The crowd yelled as Henry sped down the base line; the ball dropped safely between the outfielders and he raced around to second for a double. The Bears' fans began to clap rhythmically for a rally, but two men made out before the catcher singled Henry home to make the score 2-1.

Neither team got a hit through the next two innings, then the Tigers threatened in the seventh with a walk and a single. At shortstop Henry agitatedly kicked at some imaginary pebbles. Then deliberately he moved up in the infield a couple of steps. He realized he should be playing deep for the double play possibility, but he said to himself, "That next hitter's a real fast man, and I got to take away his advantage by playing up closer, maybe even too close. But I got to risk it this time."

As he hoped, the Tiger batter hit the ball sharply to shortstop. It came to Henry on a high, fast hop; he gloved the ball, swiftly whipped it across to the second baseman who threw on to first for the double play, nipping the speedy runner by a couple of steps. Henry went back to his normal position, well satisfied with his judgment. Had he been playing deep the Tigers' swift runner might well have beaten the second baseman's relay; there would have been men on first and third with one out instead of just a man on third with two out. The gamble, a good one, had paid off. And the next batter struck out to end the inning.

The Tigers still led by 2-1 when the Bears came to bat in the top half of the ninth inning. It was a well-played, tight ball game, especially for one involving sandlot youngsters. The Tiger pitcher retired the first man to face him in the ninth, but the next man singled, putting the tying run on base. Up to the plate, the shouts of the crowd trailing him, strode Henry Aaron.

"C'mon Henry, lose one!" he heard.

"All the way, Henry! All the way."

He tapped the end of the bat on the plate, then leaned back and waited, unblinking eyes calmly appraising the pitcher. Hardly moving a muscle, he waited there while the Tiger hurler threw a fast ball past him for a strike, then missed the plate with two curves. Henry guessed that a fast ball was due next, and, though an observer would have had to watch him closely to notice, his eyes narrowed just a bit, and the shoulder muscles rippled just a little as he cocked the bat perhaps an inch more sharply.

The fast ball came, chest high over the inside corner of the plate. Henry uncoiled, the bat cut the air like a whip and the ball jumped on a rising line to left field. The resounding crack of the bat told the fans the story —they were on their feet cheering wildly before the ball sailed into the left field bleachers for a home run.

The blow gave the Bears a 3-2 lead, which they held to win the game.

Winning games spectacularly was typical of Henry in his career with the sandlot Mobile Bears. Through the summer of 1950 he amazed and entertained the baseball fans of Mobile, young and old alike, with his fence-busting hitting. More and more older fans came to watch the Mobile Bears play as word spread of the precocious sixteen-year-old shortstop.

But soon—too soon it seemed to Henry—the summer was over and school re-opened. Baseball was his burning ambition now, and he longed for his school days to be over so that he might concentrate on pursuing what he now knew must be his career.

Astutely, his mother noticed a new restlessness in her son that winter. "You got to buckle down, boy," she said to him quietly one evening. She stood over the white porcelain sink, washing the supper dishes, while Henry sat at the kitchen table, schoolbooks open but unread before him. His mother half turned to him as she began scrubbing a big aluminum pot. "You expect to get into college the way you been doing in school?" she said.

"Ain't goin' to college," Henry replied.

She bit her lip, though she had known in her heart this would likely be his reply. "When you decide this?"

"I don't know. I just decided, that's all. No use kidding, Mom, college ain't for me."

"You weren't talking that way last year, before you began playing baseball with that Bears team. Last year you were talking pretty big about going to college and being somebody someday. Somebody on that baseball team been putting nonsense in your head boy? You know what I mean!"

"Nobody put nothin' in my head that wasn't there before," Henry said. "I'm gonna be somebody, Mom, you'll see, but there just ain't no sense in foolin' ourselves about me and college, that's all. It ain't in me to go. I'm an athlete, not a brain, and if I'm gonna be anybody that's what I got to be—a professional athlete, a baseball player."

Estella Aaron didn't give up. "They give college scholarships for athletes, don't they?" she said.

"Not much from Central High they don't. Even if they did it probably would be for basketball or football. Maybe baseball, if we had a baseball team, which we don't. All I play at Central is softball, and they ain't giving away any scholarships for that."

His mother frowned. Quietly she began stacking the dishes in a wood closet over the sink. Then she said, "You ain't thinking of quitting school now, are you Henry?"

"No," he sighed. "But you might as well know Mom it's just 'cause you and Pop want me to go that I'm goin'. If it was up to me I'd as soon quit now and get started with one of them semi-pro teams."

She shook her head. "You talk stubborn as a mule when it comes to that baseball playing," she said. She turned around and squinted at him hard. "You really —I mean *really* think you got a chance to be a baseball

21

player in them big leagues with men like Jackie Robinson and like that?"

Henry squirmed in his chair. "I—I don't know, Mom. You put it like that, I just don't know. All I know is I'd sure like to try, and I think maybe I could make it."

She nodded. "Well, meantime nobody's been around here asking for you to sign no contract. So until they do, I think you better begin reading those schoolbooks a little more. Just in case, you know." Her voice had just a touch of tease in it, but Henry didn't hear her say to herself, as she turned back to her work, "Sure give the folks around something to talk about, though, if my boy becomes a famous ballplayer."

Winter was a routine of schoolwork and chores around the neighborhood for Henry. Work was more than a means to personal luxuries now, like saving up to go to ball games; work meant a few extra dollars for the Aaron family, which, with the addition of new-born Edward that year, numbered seven children, four boys and three girls.

Football and basketball helped break the routine, but to Henry they were unsatisfactory substitutes for baseball. He played guard on the Central High football team, though he weighed only 150 pounds, and starred at forward on the basketball team. On the week ends, between odd jobs, he joined the neighborhood boys on the sandlots and in the schoolyard, but to Henry it was all marking time until spring came again and brought the sound of a connecting bat and solid smack of a baseball against the leather glove.

With Mobile's early spring came Henry's seventeenth birthday, and with it a kind of sobering realization that as the second oldest child in the large family he perhaps should hedge a bit on a baseball career. He was sitting in the Hartwell Field bleachers one March day, watching the Dodgers and the Phillies playing an exhibition game, the worry of responsibility on his mind. As he watched the graceful professionalism of such Phillies as Richie Ashburn and Curt Simmons and the Dodgers' Gil Hodges, Pee Wee Reese, Jackie Robinson and the rest, Henry realized that he had a long hard row to hoe before becoming a major league baseball player.

At the crowded, cheerfully noisy dinner table that evening only he was silent. He remained at the table after all the others had gone, and sat, watching his mother clear away the dirty dishes and begin washing them. He liked to sit and watch her like that; it seemed his mother was always washing dishes in that big household. She spoke finally, breaking the silence.

"You got something on your mind, boy?" she said quietly.

He hesitated. "Yeah. Kind of."

"You want to quit school, boy?"

"Yes—and no."

"Don't 'Yes and no' me, Henry. You got something you want to say, say it. You ain't no baby anymore."

"Mom, it's like we talked about last year. That college business don't make sense. Now you know I want to be a baseball player, and I think maybe I got a good chance to be one. But if I ain't gonna make it, then I think I oughta get out of Central and switch over to a trade school, like the Allen Institute."

"And wind up in the shipyards like your Daddy, or maybe worse."

"Since when is workin' in the shipyards something bad?"

"Oh it ain't bad. We can thank the Lord we had the shipyards all these years. We always had food for the children and a roof over our heads and money comin' in every week on payday. But there ain't no future in that, boy. You ask your Daddy about that, if there's any future in the shipyards. It was fine, fine in our time, boy, workin' in the shipyards. Workin' anywheres for a decent livin' week after week. But a boy's got a chance for more today, can't you see that? He don't have to take any old job they want to hire him for. He can go to college, and be a professional man, even if he does come from Toulminville." She was breathing hard now, excited from the exertions of what was for her a long speech.

Henry hung his head. But his lips were set hard, and in the end he convinced his mother and father that he should enroll in the Allen Institute while trying and praying for a career in baseball.

In late spring the Mobile Bears reactivated their exhibition schedule. This time, however, with the players older and more experienced after their fine season of

24

1950, the Bears decided to play exhibitions against professional teams from the National Negro League, spawning grounds at that time for such major leaguers as Jackie Robinson, Roy Campanella, Luke Easter, Larry Doby and many others.

It was an ambitious project, but the Mobile Bears admittedly were the best sandlot team in the area, and the Negro clubs were happy enough to play against any team that could draw crowds the way the Bears did in Mobile.

Henry was quick to realize the opportunity open to him.

"I got to play extra good against those pros," he said to his older brother Herbert one night, discussing the Bears' plans with him. "That's the next step for me, I think, playing with a team like the Monarchs or the Clowns."

"But wouldn't you be better off trying out for one of the major league farm teams?" his brother asked. "I heard they got tryout camps for amateur players."

Henry shook his head. "Even if I made it, I think I could maybe get buried in the minors. But if you can break in right from a good pro colored team you got a better chance to attract attention, maybe go right to the higher minors."

His brother shrugged. "You know better than me about that. I just hope you make it, that's all."

"I'll make it," Henry said grimly.

His opportunity was slow in coming, however. Through midsummer the Bears had occasion to play

25

barely half a dozen games against teams from the Negro League. Henry played well enough, at times even spectacularly, but in these few games he showed very little evidence of professional potential to attract attention.

Then, toward the end of August 1951 the Bears were invited to play a two-game set against the Indianapolis Clowns, who had a couple of open dates and preferred to remain active, their livelihood depending to some extent on the gross receipts of total games played during a season. The Bears leaped at the challenge, none with more determination and spirit than Henry Aaron. This, he knew, could be his big chance to impress shrewd, important Sid Pollet, owner of the Clowns. In fact, he realized with a tightening in his stomach, this could be his last chance this year to impress anybody important. This two-game series with the Clowns was indeed a crossroads.

3 . . .

It seemed to Henry he had never seen the stands so filled, even for a game on Saturday. The fans, he guessed, figured on seeing an exciting pair of ball games, though few honestly expected the Bears to win —they had lost all six of their earlier games against the pros. He prowled his shortstop position restlessly, kicking aimlessly at imaginary pebbles, waiting for the Bears' pitcher to take his final warm-ups and begin the game.

Apparent disaster quickly overtook the Bears. Their starting pitcher failed to last the first inning as the Clowns poured four runs over the plate in a barrage of hits. They continued their rampage against three more Bears' pitchers, winning the game in a rout, 12-2. The Bears' two runs were provided by Henry, hitting a bases-loaded double in the eighth inning. It was his second double of the game.

He slept fitfully that night, distressed with the Bears' poor showing and his own inability to be heroic. In his anxiety he discounted his two doubles and the fact that with his teammates not hitting there was indeed little

27

opportunity for heroism at the plate. He tossed in his bed, which he shared with his brother, alternating between dream-filled sleep and fantasy-filled wakefulness. Images ran through his young mind: he saw himself leaping into the air to turn a vicious line drive into a double play, saving tomorrow's game and bringing even the enemy Clowns to their feet in applause. Situations raced through his mind, rapidly, jerkily, like motion picture film running wild on the screen. He was running, sliding, jumping, hitting a bases-loaded homer; he was spiked making a double-play tag, but played on with the blood trickling into his shoes while the crowd murmured in awe and the old pros on the Clowns regarded him with quiet respect. Later they would shake his hand, and Sid Pollet would hire him on the spot to be the Clowns' shortstop.

He awoke in the middle of a series of explanations of how the regular Clowns' shortstop had quit or been injured or signed by a major league team—or something. In his imagery, he did not want to feel that he had taken away another man's job. He was groping for the most pleasing and plausible excuse when the alarm clock shattered the morning.

Half-remembered patches of dreams and fantasies clung to his mind as he swung his legs off the bed and began to dress. He shook them off angrily, hating himself for such story-book heroics. Baseball careers, he knew, were founded on more solid ground. In today's game he would have to play as he had never played before, yet he knew that unless some special opportunity came his way his best playing might well go for nothing.

He had set the alarm for an early hour so that he could dress and eat breakfast quietly, by himself, and slip out to the ball park. Rather than remain home in the frenetic awakening of a crowded household on a Sunday morning, he preferred to stretch out on a hard bench in the Bears' locker room and relax, and think, and hope, surrounded by the smells of leather and liniment he loved so well.

In the locker room he had fallen asleep again, dreamless and refreshing this time, when the jabbing foot of a teammate prodded him awake. He felt strangely renewed in purpose, calmly confident. He was able to laugh when his teammate kidded him: "Ain't you got no home, Henry? What you doin' sleepin' in this smelly place? Your folks finally kick your lazy hide outta the house?"

He was able to laugh, and rise from the hard bench with no stiffness in his body, and change into his uniform with the tingle of expectancy within him. It was going to be a fine day he remarked to himself as he strode out under the blue sky of Mobile that Sunday morning.

A little more than an hour later he strode to the plate for the first time. Batting third in the Bears' line-up, he came up with two out and nobody on base in the first inning. Smoothly, confidently, he lined the second pitch over the left field fence for a home run. As he

29

trotted around third he stole a look at the Clowns' bench to see whether any of the players or owner-manager Sid Pollet were watching him. He noted with satisfaction that several of them did seem to be staring at him, and, as he crossed home plate, the Clowns' catcher grunted at him, "Good bang, man!"

For three innings the Bears' 1-0 lead held, but their pitching was just not good enough to withstand the Clowns' hitters, some of whom had played professional baseball in the Negro League for many years. The Clowns scored three times in the fourth inning, and it looked like a repeat performance of the Saturday game was about to develop.

However, in the bottom half of the fourth inning the Bears rallied. Leading off, a pinch hitter for the pitcher drew a walk. After a force play, the Bears' first baseman singled, and there were men on first and third with Henry at bat. He stood almost languidly in the batter's box, utterly relaxed in appearance, but inwardly keyed up with expectancy.

The first pitch was low and outside, and he resisted the urgency pulsing in his wrists. He swung at the next pitch, fouling it off. The next one was a slow curve; he waited, timed it, then flicked his wrists. The ball leaped from his arcing bat and soared on a blurred line to left center field. Desperately the Clowns' outfielders raced for the ball, but it fell between them and bounced through into the deepest part of the ball park. Speeding around the bases, heart pounding, Henry pulled into third with a triple, and the score was tied 3-3.

He was too exhilarated by his hit and the roar of the crowd to look around now. but had he glanced at the Clowns' bench he would have noticed Sid Pollet leaning forward now, eyes bright and wide, lips curved in a smile. A moment later Henry scored on a fly ball and the Bears took the lead 4-3.

The game broke down into a hitting contest, pitchers on both teams shuttling in and out under the constant barrage. In the sixth inning Henry got his third straight hit, a single, starting a rally good for two runs. Coming to bat in the bottom of the ninth inning, the Bears losing 9-7, Henry was convinced that he needed some final explosion to stand a chance of influencing the Clowns' owner. He was due to bat fifth in this, the Bears' final turn at bat, and he prayed desperately that he would get a chance, that two men would reach base safely. He would not be stopped if he got that final chance, he vowed silently.

His hopes soared, then plummeted as the first man singled and the next one promptly hit into a double play. He groaned and closed his eyes. The next man walked, and as Henry got off the bench to kneel in the on-deck circle, he called to his teammate at the plate, "Get on, man! Get on! Save me a lick! Let him hit you —anything! Just get on!"

His teammate grinned, took a ball, fouled off a couple of pitches, then singled. Henry almost leaped into the air on the way to the batter's box. He dug in, then

31

backed out, bent over and rubbed dirt on his hands, giving himself a moment's time to force down the rising excitement. Don't get anxious Henry boy, he cautioned himself. Don't go swingin' at any wild ones.

The Clowns' experienced pitcher expected just that —an over-anxious youngster eager to be a hero. He slowed up his curves and hung them just off the outside corner, figuring Henry would be reaching out in his anxiety. But Henry leaned over, then leaned back again, letting the pitches go by, and soon he had the pitcher in a spot, three balls and no strikes. The next pitch figured to be a fast ball right across the plate, the so-called automatic strike, and though it would be a temptation to lash out at it, he knew that as the potential winning run he should wait the pitcher out and try to get on base with a walk if he could.

Routinely, he looked down toward the third base coach—and checked a start of surprise as he saw the "hit" sign being flashed to him. The coach was letting him swing away if the pitch looked good! In a flash Henry understood why. Without vanity, he realized that given a good pitch he had the potential to win or tie the ball game with one blow; a walk to him, on the other hand, would put the burden of hitting on less able clutch hitters than he was.

Given such a vote of confidence, there was even more reason not to fail now. He steadied himself in position, dug his spikes in a fraction deeper, cocked the bat an eyelash more. The Clowns' pitcher stretched, threw— hard and true, right down the middle of the plate.

Henry put his brief lifetime of ambition into his swing. He connected, solidly; the crowd shrieked. He wanted not to look, but knew he had to follow the flight of the ball to run smartly. He saw it arc high to left field as he churned down the first base line, and watched, rounding the bag, heart in his throat, as the ball disappeared behind the left field fence. A game-winning home run.

The stands went wild, paper cups and scraps soared in the air like confetti. His teammates clapped and cheered, all of them standing in front of the bench. As he rounded third base in a fast trot, the Clowns' third baseman patted his back in a sporting gesture of praise.

Henry dared not look at the Clowns' bench, but Sid Pollet was there, shaking his head in admiration.

In the locker room later he was still shaking hands with teammates when Pollet walked in. The Clowns' manager was not a man to waste time.

"Aaron, how'd you like to play shortstop for the Clowns?" he said.

Henry closed his eyes. It was just like in the dreams. He opened them again and Pollet was still there, real. "I'd like that just fine, Mr. Pollet," he said.

4 . . .

The Negro National League had seen nothing like him in a long time. Many great Negro ballplayers had gone before him, men who had become stars in the major leagues, like Jackie Robinson and Roy Campanella; men who had been given the opportunity too late in their careers and had not quite made it, like the fabled Satchel Paige; men who were passed over by time and never got a chance at all, like Josh Gibson. But with the breaking of the color line in organized baseball by Jackie Robinson in 1946 the exodus of qualified Negroes from the Negro League had steadily accelerated, and the minor leagues became increasingly the normal avenues of traffic for aspiring Negro ballplayers. So that by the twilight of the 1951 season an outstanding youngster like Henry Aaron was much more a phenomenon in the Negro League than he would have been five or six years earlier.

He did not really break loose until the 1952 season. For one thing, Sid Pollet did not catapult him into the starting line-up the very day he joined the Clowns, which was the day after he practically beat them single-handedly. For another, it took him the remaining weeks of the 1951 season to catch on to the vastly more experienced pitching style of the professional baseball league. The pitchers themselves were craftier than those he was accustomed to facing, and their variety and control of pitches was far superior to what he had seen with the Mobile Bears. Still, he managed to hit often enough and well enough as a rookie to please the Negro League fans and Sid Pollet, who offered him a raise in pay and a regular berth at shortstop when the season ended.

Henry was practically walking on air when he returned home with the news. Yet he was practical enough even at that point to go through with his plans for attending Allen Institute in the event a baseball career did not work out for him.

He lost little time proving that he would not need this training when the 1952 baseball season opened. Waiting until his term at the school was over, Henry joined the Clowns in Kansas City, where they were scheduled to play two games against the Monarchs. Arriving late from the railroad station, the eighteen-year-old youngster suited up just in time to take a few practice swings before the game began: Except for sandlot games at home and softball at Allen Institute, that was the extent of his spring training for the Clowns. Pollet, in fact, was not at all sure he was making the right move by allowing Henry in a league game without a few pinch-hit roles to kind of ease the path.

35

Henry's first at bat erased all doubts from the owner's mind.

Standing just a shade under the six feet he would reach in another year or two, weighing 170, about ten pounds below his eventual, mature weight, Henry stood at the plate in the first inning of the game a composed, confident young ballplayer. He let two bad pitches pass, then hit the next one into left center field for a triple, scoring a teammate ahead of him. Moments later he crossed the plate on a long fly ball, giving the Clowns a 2-0 lead. Later in the game Henry added a single and a walk to the Clowns' winning cause, giving him a two-for-four first day as a Clowns regular.

By 1952 major league scouts from all the clubs were regular visitors to the Negro League games, and, as June turned to July and Henry became the hitting terror of the league, the scouts camped on his trail. They never announced their presence, but somehow the ballplayers had a feeling when they were in the crowd, and several of the players even recognized some of the scouts, tipping off their teammates. It was Sid Pollet himself who told Henry the major league scouts were watching him.

"Got a couple nibbles already from the Phillies and the Giants," Pollet told him one day. "But nothing worth while yet."

"How about me?" Henry asked. "Can't I make any choice?"

Pollet nodded. "Don't worry. I'll get the best deal possible for both of us."

By mid-July Henry was batting .450, and the bidding for him narrowed to the Giants and the Braves, then in their final year at Boston before moving to Milwaukee. While the Braves seemed to be vacillating, the Giants came forward with a definite, final offer to buy Henry's contract and ship him to their Sioux City, Iowa, farm club. Their purchase price was satisfactory to Pollet, but neither he nor Henry were entirely happy with the salary offer.

The Clowns were in Buffalo one day in mid-July when Pollet said to Henry, "Let's get this over and done with once and for all. You should be playing in regular organized baseball and I want to help put you there. What do you say about that Giant deal?"

Henry thought a moment. "Mr. Pollet," he said finally, "I just can't tell you how I feel exactly. Playing in the regular leagues is something I dreamed about for a long time, and now it's here for the asking I thought I'd feel something more. I don't know, excited. I am excited, and grateful, don't get me wrong. But somehow I got the feeling they ain't paying enough money, taking advantage knowing how bad I'd like to sign with them."

Pollet stared at him. "That's more words than I heard you say since I know you. And I think maybe you're right, too. So tell you what. Suppose we call the Braves and give 'em one more chance. If they don't come up with an offer by seven o'clock tomorrow night, we sign with the Giants. Okay?"

"Okay," Henry said.

The following day was overcast, and intermittent drizzle fell in the morning, but Braves' scout Dewey Griggs journeyed to Buffalo to see whether Henry Aaron was worth buying from the Clowns. They were willing enough to better the Giants' salary offer without a further look, but they hesitated at Sid Pollet's demands: $2500 down and another $7500 a month later if Henry made good. If not, he could be returned to the Clowns, but the $2500 was non-refundable.

The game that day was delayed by rain, and the field was a near quagmire when it finally did get under way. Hat pulled low over his eyes against the mist, Griggs sat up in the stands and kept his eyes glued to Henry throughout the day. By the time the game ended it was six o'clock, just an hour before Pollet's deadline. Griggs taxied back to his hotel and put in a call to Boston, to the private number of John Quinn, general manager of the Braves.

"I saw that Aaron kid at Buffalo today," he reported.

"So," Quinn responded, "what do you think, can he play short?"

"Tell you the truth," Griggs said, "the field was so wet I couldn't tell for sure. But I can tell you this. He's worth twenty-five hundred dollars just for his swing."

"All right," Quinn said. "Sign him."

Griggs hung up, phoned the Clowns' hotel. Pollet answered the switchboard's ring. "Oh, it's you Griggs," he said. "We'd about given you up, Henry and me. We were about to call the Giants and say okay."

"Don't do it. I'll be right over," Griggs said. "I got the okay from the boss just now."

The next two days were a vague whirlwind of contract signings, calls to home, congratulations from his teammates and a long talk with scout Griggs. Then Henry was on a train bound for Eau Claire, Wisconsin, in the Northern League. It was only there on the train, alone, the reality of his making it to organized baseball facing him, that he allowed himself the first flicker of fear. Not of his ability. He felt deep within that he had the ability and the purpose to rise through the minor leagues to the Braves themselves or some other major league team. But he had cause for uneasiness elsewhere. Tomorrow he would be a Negro ballplayer on a white team in a white league up North. It was a subject distasteful even to his thoughts, but the subject had cropped up inevitably among the Clowns, and he had learned, not without some surprise, that at times a Negro faced greater problems in the North than in the South.

"In the South," a teammate once told him, "you know where you can go and where you can't. What you can do and what you can't. Now you travel around up North and sometimes you find you can't go where you thought you could. Let me tell you, boy, that's a worse feelin' than the other way."

Henry recalled those words now, and other words, too, of problems and situations facing a Negro ballplayer that trickled down from organized baseball to the Negro League. The color line may have been officially broken on the ball field, but the word was that a Negro ballplayer who thought that was the end of discrimination against him was in for a bad time. Hostility was still there, even among teammates and sports reporters.

"Best you keep your mouth shut and mind your own business," Henry had been advised by a teammate before leaving. "You'll find a lot of whites expect a kid like you, coming from the South especially, to act like the end man in a minstrel show, know what I mean?"

Henry did not know, exactly, but he had a good idea. Being eighteen, he had reason to worry about getting along. All he could do, he figured, was be careful, and see how things went. He tried to shake the doubts and misgivings from his mind and replace them with the good things that had come and would come his way. Finally, as the train roared northward in the night toward Eau Claire, he retreated into sleep.

He found in Eau Claire, pleasantly enough, that baseball would be his primary battle. If, at times, teammates directed at him sullen stares and what appeared to be angry mutterings, he felt that they were more the manifestations of Class C competition than personal antagonism. Here, Henry reasoned with a clarity beyond his years, were a group of young ballplayers fighting for their professional life, struggling to rise up the ladder toward the major leagues. He knew that in each man, underlying his desire to win as a team, was the anxious knowledge that when a teammate looked exceptionally good it dulled some of his own glitter.

Henry was certainly exceptionally good. A week after reporting to Eau Claire he was named to the league's All-Star team. He finished the season with a .336 batting average and was selected Rookie of the Year in the Northern League. The Braves promptly promoted him to a Class A farm team, the Jacksonville Tars of the Sally (South Atlantic) League.

This quick vote of confidence given him by the Braves helped his ego tremendously. It was in effect a testimonial of recognition that his play at Eau Claire had been more than good, that the Braves' management was keeping its eye on him.

He had little illusion about the kind of welcome he could expect in Jacksonville. He knew that he would be breaking the color barrier, that no Negro ever had played in the Sally League before. He would be facing a double-barrelled challenge.

5...

Henry Aaron stood at the plate under the hot Florida sun, opening day of the 1953 season, and tried not to listen to the chorus of jeers from the stands. If this is what I get from the home team fans, he thought fleetingly, what can I expect around the rest of the league? Then he shut out everything but the immediate problem—the first pitch due from Corky Valentine, pitcher for the Columbia, South Carolina, team, later pitcher for the Cincinnati Reds.

Columbia, the 1952 Sally League champions, was favored to repeat, and Valentine figured to be its leading hurler. The young pitcher, as it turned out, was top man in the league, but at the moment he looked nothing like it as Henry ripped into his fast ball and banged it off the left field wall for a double, scoring teammate Horace Garner from first. Henry noted, with some satisfaction, that a few half-hearted cheers could be heard among the jeers that still echoed in the grandstand.

Valentine retired the Tars without further scoring in the opening inning, and, with Ray Crone, later a

Braves pitcher, on the mound for Jacksonville, the game settled down into a pitchers' battle. For six innings Crone held his 1-0 lead, then a single by Lew Davis and a homer by Jim Bolger in the seventh gave Columbia a one-run margin. Jacksonville came back with a run in the eighth to tie the score, but two more runs by Columbia in the top half of the ninth made the score 4-2.

Garner opened the Tars' ninth by striking out, and the fans groaned. Rising leisurely and calmly from the on-deck circle, Henry walked up to the plate. Hitless in two attempts after his opening-inning double, he had heard the jeers renewed with added vigor. His face was impassive as he dug into the batter's box, bat held slightly away from his body. In spring training manager Ben Geraghty had started to tamper with that stance, thinking that Henry held the bat too far out in front, but when he saw how the youngster's powerful wrists whipped the bat around, he wisely backed off. "I'd have to be crazy to tamper with that swing," he told one of his coaches.

Now Henry stood in the batter's box on opening day, and through the jeers of the crowd he heard his teammates on the bench exhort him to get a rally going.

"Get ahold of one, Hank boy!" he heard one call.

He liked that, being called "Hank." Somehow it made him feel accepted—accepted as just another ballplayer on the club, which was precisely the way he wanted it. Let the fans boo at him, he thought grimly. All I care about is what goes on here on the ball field.

43

The Columbia right-hander on the mound coiled into a windup, came around and spun a fast curve that was too wide, for ball one. Henry let the next pitch go by for a strike. The next serve was a fast ball over the inside corner; he swung and pulled it just fair inside third base, the ball rolled into the corner and he pulled into second base standing up for a double.

"Attaway, Hank!" came a cry from the Jacksonville bench.

He felt good. He felt proud. Hank—he couldn't recall anyone calling him by that name in Mobile, not regularly anyway, but he resolved that he was going to be known as Hank from then on.

He took his lead off second as third baseman Bill Porter came up to bat. Valentine stretched, looked back at second as Hank widened his lead, pitched to the plate, and Porter looped a single to right field. Holding up several moments to make sure the looping fly ball could not be caught, Hank had to put on extra speed to score. He came home in a dust-raising slide, beating the outfielder's throw by an eyelash.

That made the score 4-3, with Porter racing to second on the play at the plate. Fired up now, the Tars jumped on Valentine for successive singles, tying the score; then a double off relief pitcher John Bebber drove home the winning run for a 5-4 Jacksonville victory.

In the clubhouse later the Tars' morale was high: there was loud laughter and the sounds of spirited horseplay above the clanging of locker doors and the hiss of the showers. It augured well to beat the champions from Columbia and their best pitcher on opening day. Dressing in front of his locker, Hank was gratified to find that though there was general diffidence toward him from his teammates—and he understood and accepted it—a few did stop by and pat him on the back for his important role in the victory.

He was not entirely satisfied with his situation on the Tars, however. Opening day had found him at a strange position, second base, with Felix Mantilla, later to be a teammate on the Braves, the regular Tar shortstop.

Manager Geraghty had explained it to him. "Felix won't hit within fifty points of you," he predicted accurately, "but he plays a better shortstop. And what I need is a second baseman. Let's face it, Hank, you didn't win a spot on this club because of your glove. I think in a month I can have you playing second as well as you ever played shortstop."

Hank wasn't so sure, but he threw himself into the new position with energy. Geraghty gave him every opportunity to take extra fielding practice, and he used it to good purpose. He had to learn, all over again, the pivot at second base for the double play, how to play the area for left- and right-hand batters, taking the throw from the catcher on attempted steals, and a host of other details, the skills that added up to the difference between an adequate second baseman and an outstanding one.

When the month Geraghty figured on had passed,

Hank was an adequate second baseman, and it appeared quite likely that he would never be more than just that. Still, the infield of Joe Andrews at first base, Hank at second, Mantilla at shortstop, and Bill Porter and Harry Warner sharing third came to be considered just about the finest in the Sally League.

Adding weight to that status was Hank's hitting, which more than compensated for his merely adequate fielding. By the end of May in that 1953 season neither Geraghty, the fans, nor Hank's teammates cared too much about his fielding. He was tearing apart the league's pitchers with his bat, leading all hitters in every department, breaking up ball games with dramatic hits just the way he had done it with the Mobile Bears. And in the same way the fans all over the league were filling the ball parks to see this nineteen-year-old phenomenon hit.

Through it all Hank searched for a way to adjust as a human being. On the field his status as a ballplayer was secure: the jeers by now were far from non-existent, but they were fewer and growing even scarcer with each day. Off the field was another matter; he could not eat and sleep with his teammates, and the light banter of the locker room drifted around him and through him. He had expected nothing more and perhaps less. He became, in self-protection, laconic in speech; garrulous he never had been, now he retired into greater silence. He became a great sleeper. On the long bus rides he invariably fell promptly to sleep and had to be awakened at his destination by a teammate. It became a joke with the Tars.

"Ol' Hank can fall asleep standing up," the players kidded.

"Most relaxed man I ever saw," another teammate laughed. "He even looks like he's asleep at the plate. Till the ball comes. Then wham!"

Hank let the humor stand. He was pleased with it in fact. It could have been worse. He was determined, as a pioneer Negro in the league—a deep South league at that—to avoid trouble, and if the innocent image he seemed to portray was that of a happy-go-lucky guy, it was fine with him. He'd keep it that way.

He could in fact embellish it, for he had a dry, dead-pan humor, and, using it sparingly, he rounded out the image he thought everyone around him liked the best. It worked fine in Jacksonville. Later, however, Hank would have cause to regret it.

As the season rolled into July the Sally League race narrowed down to three clubs: Jacksonville, Columbia and Columbus, Georgia. The rest of the league was far back, comprising Savannah, Macon and Augusta, all in Georgia, Charleston, South Carolina, and Montgomery, Alabama.

In mid-July Columbus came to Jacksonville for a three-game series, trailing the league-leading Tars by five games and the second place Columbians by four. They knew they had to win at least two of the three games to remain seriously in contention. Practically by himself, Hank demolished their chances for the season.

47

Ron Kump was his first victim. The Columbus pitcher was riding along in the series opener with a 3-1 lead. Then, weakening in the eighth inning, he walked a man, the next man singled and Hank belted a game-winning homer.

In the second game Hank began the scoring in the first inning when he tripled, then scored on a single. He wasted a single in the third inning, but a bases-loaded double in the sixth turned the score around from 4-2 Columbus to 5-4 Jacksonville. The determined visitors knocked out Tar pitcher Everett Lively in the seventh, however, regaining the lead, 7-5.

The bottom of the ninth came up that way, with Tom Keating on the mound for Columbus. He got the first man, but Mantilla singled, outfielder Jim Frey walked and up to the plate came Hank.

Joe Ossola, the Columbus catcher, trotted out to the pitcher's mound and there was a hurried conference. "Whattaya think?" he said to Keating. "Better keep 'em low and away on this guy. He gets ahold of one it's all over."

Keating nodded. "There's no book on him. I ain't found a pitch yet he can't hit. I asked around, too. Nobody has anything."

"Well, let's try all curves anyway, over the outside."

Keating nodded and turned away, rubbing up the ball, as Ossola ran back behind the plate.

With runners at first and second Keating went into a stretch and delivered the first pitch. The curve broke good over the outside corner and Hank took it for a called strike. Keating continued the curves, missing twice, making Hank foul one off. Two balls and two strikes. Again Keating went to the outside with a curve —the pitch looked too far out and would have been a ball, but Hank swung, and with his powerful wrists pulled the outside pitch to left field, sent it rising up into the left field stands for a home run. Allowing himself a smile at the cheers from the stands, he trotted around the bases and crossed the plate with the winning run.

Chief Bender, former major league pitching great and now manager of the Columbus team, knew that his back was to the wall. He had to win the series finale to remain in contention. He started Doug Clark, his top pitcher, and readied a battery of relief pitchers in the bull pen, planning to use them all if necessary. Hank did make it necessary, continuing his hitting rampage.

Again he began the Tars' offensive, lining a double to left field in the first inning. Porter drove him home with a single and Jacksonville was on the way. In the third inning, with the score tied 1-1, Hank drove home two runs with a second straight double, knocking out Clark. Keating came in for Columbus, stopped the rally but was knocked out himself two innings later on a walk, two singles and Hank's third home run in three days. The score was now 7-3 Jacksonville, with their pitcher Crone breezing along.

Roland Hubbard was Hank's final victim. The relief pitcher, who had come in to replace Keating, did well enough until the eighth inning, but with two out he

49

BLAIRSVILLE SENIOR HIGH SCHOOL
BLAIRSVILLE, PENNA.

walked Frey, giving Hank a last chance at bat. Hubbard's technique was to pitch him in tight, brushing him away from the plate. The second pitch made Hank duck and fall to the ground. He rose slowly, dusting dirt from his hands. Then he hit the next pitch on a line to left center field for a double, making the score 8-3. Out came Hubbard, but the game was beyond reach. The final score was 10-3, and, by beating Columbus three straight, the Tars had sent them eight games behind, a blow from which they never recovered. They finished in third place, twenty-six games behind.

Now there were only Jacksonville and Columbia in the race. The two teams battled heroically through August and into September, alternating leads, never more than three games separating them. Hitting consistently at about the .350 mark, Hank led the Tars' attack, and though he also led the league's second basemen in errors, manager Geraghty remarked that he certainly batted in many more runs than he might have allowed to score through his misplays.

In mid-September the Tars came out of a three-game sweep in Charleston one game behind Columbia and with a four-game set due next against the league-leaders—two double-headers in two days due to rained-out games earlier in the season. The series loomed a climactic one, with the pressure on the Tars; a split of the four games, with the season's end barely a week away, would benefit only the Columbians' one-game lead. The Tars, therefore, knew they had to win at least three games to regain the lead. A three-game win by Columbia, on the other hand, would give them a three-game lead and practically assure them the league pennant.

On the bus trip from Charleston the keyed-up Jacksonville players chattered nervously, were perhaps overly boisterous. Hank, as usual, slept. "How can he sleep with those two double-headers coming up?" one of the Tars exclaimed. "Don't he know we blow the season if we lose them double-headers?"

Manager Geraghty overheard. "I wouldn't be surprised if he didn't even know we were in second place," he said. "Though I got a hunch he knows exactly where we stand. But what's he got to worry about? Hanks knows he's gonna get his share of hits in those double-headers, and probably more than his share. That's more than you can be sure of, so stop squawkin'."

As the bus pulled up at the Columbia ball park Geraghty mentally crossed his fingers on his assessment of Hank's value in the next two days. The youngster had come through consistently, even amazingly, all season long. Without him, Geraghty knew, the Tars would have been a flop. He knew too that the pressure on the youngster was tremendous, on and off the field, and that a let-down, particularly at the tail end of the season, was only to be expected. Geraghty hoped fervently that Hank would keep going strong through the two double-headers. If he slumped now, the Tars were finished.

He shook Hank awake as the other players began

filing out of the bus. "We're here, kid, this is it," he said.

Hanks eyes flickered open. He yawned, stretched, looked out the window. "Who they starting in the first game, you know, Skipper?" he said.

"Polivka."

"Good," Hank said. "The lefty. I hit him good last time."

"Let's hope you hit him good this time," Geraghty said, half to himself, as they left the bus and walked into the ball park.

Ken Polivka was a seventeen-game winner and one of the toughest left-handers in the league, but Hank hit him that day as though he were the Tars' batting practice pitcher. The entire Jacksonville offense got only eight hits off the Columbia pitcher, but Hank got four of them: two doubles, a single, and a game-winning homer in the eighth inning, the Tars winning 4-3.

In the second half of the double-header Ray Crone of the Tars faced Maurice Fisher of Columbia. Fisher, another top hurler with sixteen victories, nevertheless suffered a similar pounding from Hank's seemingly unstoppable bat. Another close ball game was won by the Tars as the young second baseman went three-for-four, driving in four runs in the 6-4 victory.

The double win gave Jacksonville the league lead by one game, but even more, the incredible hitting of Hank Aaron gave an already fired-up team a tremendous lift. Chattering away in the locker room after the second game, the excited players could hardly wait for the next day's double-header, confident they could not be stopped.

The luckless Columbians felt the full weight of the Tars' attack the next day. Again led by Hank, who managed five hits in the two games despite being walked intentionally three times, Jacksonville battered Columbia 12-5 and 9-1. It was all over but the final statistics as far as the pennant was concerned. Jacksonville now had a three-game lead and had destroyed the morale of its only competitor. The final standings had Jacksonville on top by two and one-half games.

There is no World Series in the minor leagues, but within each league there is a four-team playoff for a championship. Jacksonville first would play fourth-place Savannah, Columbia would play third-place Columbus in best three-out-of-five series. Then the winners would meet in a championship playoff, best four games out of seven. As expected, Jacksonville and Columbia won their first playoffs and met for the championship.

This time the winner's role was reversed. Hank was his usual rampaging self at bat, but it was not enough. In a fiercely played series that went the limit of seven games, Columbia won the championship, four games to three.

Just about all the hitting championships possible were the personal property of Hank, however. He led the league in batting average with .362, in runs batted in with 125, and led also in runs scored, total hits and doubles. In home runs and triples he was second. It came as a surprise to nobody when Hank was voted the Most Valuable Player in the South Atlantic League. He had broken the color line in the league with a resounding bang. By season's end what few jeers were heard were more than outweighed by the chorus of cheers that greeted his arrival at the plate.

It was a happy fall for Hank. After the playoffs, his mother and father came down to Jacksonville to see their young son married. Still several months shy of twenty, Hank that October married Barbara Lucas, a Jacksonville girl he met at a dance during the summer. After a simple ceremony and a short honeymoon the newlyweds returned to Mobile, where Hank's wife would remain while he went to play winter baseball with Caguas-Guayama in the Puerto Rican League. There, under manager Mickey Owen, former Brooklyn Dodger catcher, Hank rubbed elbows for the first time with major leaguers, many of whom played ball in the Caribbean to keep in shape and earn extra money. Hank not only held up well in competition with them, but wound up third in the league in batting with a .322 average. Among his teammates on Caguas-Guayama, which won the Puerto Rican League title, were major leaguers Jim Rivera of the White Sox and Ruben Gomez of the Giants, and such future major league talent as Luis Arroyo, Charley Neal, Brooks Lawrence, Felix Mantilla and Vic Power.

The Caribbean baseball season ended late in February, practically in time to begin major league spring training. Primed and ready to go, his bat still hot from winter baseball, Hank waited eagerly for some word from the Braves.

6...

He could not know it of course, but Hank was very much in the thoughts of the Braves' management that winter of 1953-54. While he was playing ball under the warm Puerto Rican sun, the team's top executives were meeting in their offices under the snow-covered roof of Milwaukee's County Stadium. Manager Charley Grimm stood at one of the large windows, rubbing away at the foggy condensation so he could look down at the white street below. Behind a large walnut desk owner Lou Perini swung lazily in a leather swivel chair. In other chairs were seated general manager John Quinn, John Mullen, director of the Braves' minor league operations, chief scout Jack Zeller, several other scouts and important front office members. A soft blue cloud of cigar smoke drifted along the white ceiling. It was just a few days after New Year's, 1954.

Manager Grimm turned from his position at the window. "Snowing like mad down there," he said, breaking a momentary silence in the room. He looked then at general manager Quinn. "John, what about this kid

Aaron? Maybe it's a good idea to bring him up for a look in spring training. Reports on him are good."

Quinn nodded. "Not too much as a second baseman, but he can hit. I gather he's a couple years away yet."

"A kid can hit like him," Grimm said, "I got the feeling maybe we remake him into an outfielder. Especially since we got a good glove man like Danny O'Connell in that Pirate trade last week."

"Good point," owner Perini put in. "O'Connell can handle second base for us for a long time. He's what, twenty-six?"

"Right," said Grimm. "And I'll tell you something else. Except for Bruton, our outfield ain't so young. Even if we make that deal with the Giants to get Bobby Thomson, he's thirty, maybe thirty-one. Pafko is thirty-five. This Aaron kid ain't quite twenty and he's a right-handed hitter, which we could use." Grimm looked around the room at the other men. "Anybody else got ideas along the same lines?"

"How about Aaron's running?" one of the scouts said. "They say he runs bad. On his heels. Is he fast enough for the outfield?"

"They say he covers ground good though," Grimm maintained. "Lopes around, like an antelope. Runs the bases good enough too."

"But the kid never played the outfield at all before," another scout said.

"So neither did Mickey Mantle till the Yankees put him there. I hear he dropped more than a couple fly balls, too, his first year up. But he's paying off now."

Perini cleared his throat loudly, drawing their attention back to him. "Charley, you got an idea maybe Aaron's good enough to be brought up to the Braves this year?"

Grimm shook his head. "Uh-uh. Another year, maybe even two, in Triple A ball before he's ready for big league pitching."

"Toledo?" Quinn, the general manager, offered.

"Just the spot," Grimm agreed.

Word came at last, in the waning days of the Caribbean season. He was invited to join the Braves in spring training; but he was placed on the roster of the Toledo club of the American Association.

He knew he should feel elation, yet there was a sinking feeling in the pit of his stomach. He had dared hope for more. Manager Owen tried to argue him out of his disappointment. "Listen, kid, you're jumping to Triple A ball, that's a man's league, one step below the majors. Heck, you only got two seasons of organized ball behind you. Don't be so impatient!"

"I know you're right," Hank said. "But I feel ready now. I don't want to get lost in the minor leagues after coming so close . . ."

"A guy who hits like you don't get lost," Owen said. "How do you know what the Braves got in mind for you?"

"That's just it, I don't know, and that's what I'm afraid of," Hank admitted.

He was dimly aware that somewhere in Milwaukee

the conferences that had decided his fate were also deciding the fates not only of the Braves' minor league players but their regulars, too. And though as a youngster in the organization he knew vaguely that the Braves, after many poor years in Boston, had moved to Milwaukee in 1953, he was generally unaware of the fantastic welcome accorded the team by the Milwaukee citizens.

Hank was soon to move into the most enthusiastically supported team in the major leagues. The Dodgers, then still in Brooklyn, were supposed to have the most rabid fans in baseball, but even their support paled beside the adulation heaped upon the members of the Braves.

The city's political leaders as well as its citizens had hoped wildly that the Braves would move to Milwaukee, and when they did, not only the city but seemingly the entire state of Wisconsin went big league. "The Braves put us on the country's map," one citizen remarked in 1953, reflecting the mood of thousands of Milwaukeeans. A new civic pride seemed to overtake everything and everybody. A business firm in Beloit, advertising for personnel for its plant, said, "Only ninety miles from County Stadium." At a striking bakery in Milwaukee a picket carried a sign, "We're a big league town. We want big league wages."

A new generation of fans who had never seen a big league baseball game suddenly came into being. Milwaukee had housed the minor league Brewers team until the Braves moved in, but never had there been a comparative movement of team support. At a time when major league attendance was ranging from good to much less than fair, the Milwaukee fans broke every record in the league. Reserved seats at County Stadium were sold out for the 1953 season far in advance. Business firms bought blocks of hundreds of tickets for employees and guests; the record was a purchase of 7500 seats by one firm for a Sunday double-header.

All through the team's first season in Milwaukee the fans showered the players with gifts. Outstanding ballplayers on most clubs are given a "Day" sometime in their careers, and are given gifts. In Milwaukee the "Day" lasted all the 1953 season and for all players. Andy Pafko, voted the fans the most poular player, received a Cadillac and thousands of dollars in other gifts. Pitcher Warren Spahn got a tractor for his farm Sid Gordon got a $1000 bond and dozens of other valuable gifts. Rookie Bill Bruton was given three rooms of furniture and a down payment on a house. All the players shared in the generosity and enthusiasm of small Milwaukee business firms, which provided the entire team with such items as free gasoline, milk, butter, eggs, tailoring services, haberdashery, bread, frozen food and whatnot all season long.

The fans were irrepressible, matching in insanity the stories that had favored the Brooklyn Dodger fans for so many years. In County Stadium one night a man fell and cut open his head. Rushing to the park nurse, blood streaming down his face, he asked for first aid quickly.

"You'll need stitches in that wound," she said, examining the cut.

"Never mind stitches," the man said. "Just bandage it up fast. I got to get back and watch the rest of the game."

On opening day of the 1953 season the Braves beat Cincinnati 2-0, then flew back to Milwaukee to open the season at home in County Stadium. Ten thousand frantically cheering fans met them at the airport. The team nobody had wanted to see in Boston the year before, everybody wanted to see now in Milwaukee.

Nothing could keep the fans away. The morning of one scheduled double-header in May it poured for hours, yet more than five thousand die-hard partisans stood in line in the rain hoping the weather would clear and the games be played. In May, too, a cold snap sent the temperature down to forty degrees for a night game with the Giants; the fans bundled into overcoats, brought thermos jugs of hot coffee and jammed the ball park solid.

Adversity only drove the incredible fans to greater lengths of loyalty; not a jeer was heard for a Milwaukee player in a slump; attendance actually rose when the team faltered. And at season's end, when the team returned home in second place—they had finished seventh the year before in Boston—the fans welcomed them with a parade befitting conquering heroes. By comparison the pennant-winning Dodgers were treated with indifference by their supposedly passionate followers.

Milwaukeeans, in fact, adopted the old cry of Dodger fans at the end of the 1953 season: "Wait till next year!"

It was into this background of confidence, enthusiasm and devoted support that Hank moved in the spring of 1954. Ticketed for a year of seasoning at Toledo come opening day, he arrived at the Braves' spring training camp in Bradenton, Florida, knowing at least he would be playing alongside and against major leaguers in the several weeks ahead.

The news that he was to be converted to an outfielder fell like a blow. He realized that his fielding was not the best, but this meant that it was considered too far below major league caliber. He didn't mind the conversion itself, except that learning a new position meant a delay in his rise to the Braves. He realized, however, that as an outfielder his long range chances were better; a team needs three outfielders but only one second baseman.

In the opening days of spring training he worked diligently at learning the outfielder's trade. While a coach or one of the players hit fly ball after fly ball, Hank ran and ran over the outfield grass bringing them down. He could of course catch a fly ball; as an infielder he had caught many a pop fly, but the skill of an outfielder, he quickly learned, depended in a great part on his snap judgment of the direction and speed of a ball as soon as it leaves the bat. He noticed, for example, that Bill Bruton was able to turn and run with

62

his back to home plate practically at the crack of the bat, then turn again at exactly the right moment, ready to catch the falling ball.

Hank's first attempts at judgment were unhappy. He circled and floundered, advanced and retreated, often missing the ball in a last-moment one-handed stab of desperation. Once, when he became entangled in his own feet and fell down, Bobby Thomson burst spontaneously into laughter. "I think maybe you ought to switch back to the infield," Thomson said, chuckling. When he saw the determination on Hank's face he added, "Don't let it throw you, kid. It takes a good couple of years to get the hang of playing the outfield. You got good instinct. You'll make it fine."

Were it not for his hitting Hank's spring training tryout would have been a complete failure. Still sharp from his Caribbean League playing, he cracked the ball with authority from opening day in Bradenton. His prowess with the bat was made even more outstanding by the fact that the regular players were out of shape and off in their timing after the winter vacation.

Manager Grimm was impressed. "But hitting against our own pitchers in intra-squad games is one thing," he said to a Milwaukee sports writer. "Hitting against the other guy's pitchers, that's something else we'll have to see."

"You mean you plan to start Aaron in one of the exhibition games?" the reporter asked.

"Why not?" Grimm said. "His fielding is coming

along pretty good, and what better place to try it out than in a real ball game. Besides, I want to see what this kid can do against the likes of Roberts, Erskine, Haddix, Maglie and them."

In early March the Dodgers came to Bradenton to open the spring exhibition series, and Hank felt a slight tremor of nervousness. He was moved to a great inner excitement at being on the same field with Jackie Robinson, Roy Campanella, Gil Hodges and Duke Snider. He felt much less hero worship for his own temporary Braves teammates, for the Dodgers were league champions when he was still a sandlotter. It was not many years since he had sat awestruck in the stands at Hartwell Field in Mobile and watched Robinson pioneer his way into organized baseball. Now a wild dream had become near-reality. There was Jackie Robinson and all the rest on the same baseball field with him, and when, during batting practice, Robinson made it a point to walk over and shake his hand, wishing him luck, Hank was overwhelmed. After this, he told himself, he could take Toledo. He felt more than ever that it would be just another brief interlude and very soon he would be wearing a Braves' uniform for keeps.

He felt a new inspiration and confidence as he trotted out to take his place in left field in the first inning. And when, batting third in the line-up, he came up to the plate for the first time, he hit Carl Erskine's first pitch for a double. As he pulled into second base standing up Robinson bluffed a tag at him and said, grin-

ning, "I didn't mean to wish you that much luck!"
Hank had the temerity at that moment to grin back
at the great Dodger star.

He got another hit in the game, which the Braves
won, and two hits in each of the next two games against
the Dodgers, who were much impressed. "I hear the
Braves are sending Aaron to Toledo," remarked pitcher
Billy Loes. "Good. I hope he winds up in the American
League. I don't think I'd like to have to pitch against
him regularly."

"That boy's gonna be murder on us in a couple
years," Roy Campanella told a New York sports writer.
"He's a natural swinger, and I don't think a pitcher's
gonna be able to find a weak spot on him once he gets
a little more experience."

Toward the end of the second week in March Hank
was batting at an amazing .400 pace, and though this
early in spring training managers usually platoon rook-
ies and tryout players, Grimm kept Hank playing full
time. "He's got plenty of time to report to Toledo,"
Grimm told questioners. "I want to see just how long
the kid can keep hitting like this."

On March 13 the Braves moved into St. Petersburg
for an exhibition series with the Yankees. Midway
through the opening game Thomson dropped a hit into
right center field, and, trying for a double, slid hard
into second base. When the dust cleared, the outfielder
was still lying on the ground, rolling in agony, holding
his right ankle. "I think it's busted!" he groaned as
players from both clubs rushed to him.

Broken it was indeed, and with it, the Braves felt, were their chances for a pennant, for Thomson had been counted on to lead the club's hitters. Who could replace him? everyone wondered. Aaron? A twenty-year-old with less than two years of organized baseball experience, and none of that playing the outfield?

It seemed an impossible choice, but manager Grimm made it. "Aaron's my left fielder for the time being," he said to incredulous Milwaukee sports writers. "He's shown me he can hit major league pitching, his fielding has been good enough and is improving daily and his arm is okay. He'll be in there when we open the season in Cincinnati."

7 . . .

Crosley Stadium in Cincinnati is not the most exciting place to open a baseball season; the crowds, at least
in the early 1950's, were neither large nor voluble for
opening day crowds and indeed the Reds had given
the fans little to be excited about. Still, for Hank Aaron
opening day at Crosley Field in 1954 was as thrilling
an event as he could recall in his lifetime. In his soft
new Braves' uniform he felt he was the luckiest kid
ever to come out of Mobile—much less Toulminville.
He stood near the batting cage at pre-game practice,
drinking in the scene of his first major league ball
game. Even in Cincinnati there was something in the
air that said to Hank this wasn't minor league baseball
—this was it, the big time, the major leagues, the only
thing that counted if baseball was inside of you the
way it was inside Hank Aaron. The cry of the hot dog
and ice cream hawkers, the "Hey! Get your scorecard
here!" the brightness of the sun, the green of the grass,
the quiet air of confidence and competence on the field,
all told him that he had arrived at that final plateau of
organized baseball, the major leagues.

He had seen his name in the line-up pinned on the dugout wall a few minutes earlier, but it still was hard to believe. He stood near the batting cage, waiting for his turn to hit, and slowly he ran his fingers over the word "Braves' and the number "44" sewn in black-trimmed red on the front of his uniform. And still he found it incredible.

After resigning himself to a year at Toledo, this all had come so suddenly—Thomson's breaking his ankle, Grimm's statement that he, Hank Aaron would not go to Toledo at all but would be the Braves' new left fielder—that he could not shake off a certain feeling of disbelief. It was, he felt, as though he was in a half-dream, and he was afraid that at any moment he would wake up and there would be Bobby Thomson standing where he was now, and he himself would be in a Toledo uniform.

Well whatever it is, he resolved, he would do his best to make good. Today, the Redlegs were starting their right-handed rookie, Art Fowler, and earlier manager Grimm had made it a point to take him aside and give him a special rundown on Fowler's style and pitching habits. "Now don't get over-anxious," Grimm warned him. "Just swing away like you did in spring training and you'll be okay."

It was his turn in the batting cage now, and he couldn't help but notice that not only some of his team-mates but some of the Redlegs too stopped what they were doing to watch him. He obliged the onlookers by smashing pitch after pitch deep to the outfield, rattling

68

the fence with a couple of drives and sending one into the grandstand on a rising line. He felt good after the practice stint, and with so many eyes on him, he forced himself to walk casually back to the dugout, as though this were something he had been doing for many years.

Grimm opened Hank at second in the batting order, behind leadoff man Bill Bruton, with Ed Mathews and Joe Adcock coming up third and fourth. He therefore had not long to wait for his first at bat when the game got under way. Bruton began by working Fowler for a walk. Hank came up, flailed away at Fowler's curves and struck out swinging. He walked back to the dugout in disgust. Next time he'd murder the ball, he promised himself. But the next time up he hit into a double play, and the next time he struck out again. The Braves were far behind when he came up for his last at bat, in the eighth inning. This time he fouled out.

In the clubhouse later, dressing quietly, he was in despair. What a terrible beginning! Who knew but what manager Grimm might not change his mind after his awful performance and promptly ship him off to Toledo! He couldn't look any of his teammates in the eye as they talked and dressed around him, though Bruton, using the locker next to his, said to him, "Tough opener, Hank, but tomorrow's another day."

He mumbled something in reply, but kept his head facing straight ahead into his locker as he dressed. He took his time, preferring to be one of the last to reach the bus that would take them to their hotel downtown. Finally, as he was ready to leave, Grimm walked over

69

to him. There were a few players left in the clubhouse, although they were out of earshot at the far end of the room. Grimm stood there for a moment, watching Hank tuck his shirt tails into his trousers, then loosely knot a tie. Then he spoke quietly, but forcefully.

"Hank, you were bad today. I ain't gonna kid you 'cause you know you were. So let's get that out of the way. But I want to tell you this, and remember it good and for a long time. If you're gonna play ball in the majors you're gonna hit up against the best pitchers there are, and you're gonna have plenty of bad days. You got to forget and start all over again tomorrow. This was your first big league game and you were trying too hard. I could see the first time you got up but I didn't want to say anything. Figured to let you get it out of your system. But there's a hundred and fifty-three games left to play, and you're my left fielder as long as you're healthy enough to walk up there with a bat. So don't push yourself and don't worry. You ain't going to Toledo if you do bad tomorrow either. You ain't going noplace but left field for the Braves. Got it?"

Hank gulped hard, nodded stiffly, eyes still staring into his locker.

"Whew!" Grimm breathed. "That's the longest speech I made since last winter's baseball writers' dinner." He clapped Hank on the shoulder. "C'mon, let's go get a thick steak."

Though the Braves lost again the next day, Hank got his first major league hit, a double that drove in two runs in the fourth inning. "That first one's always the

70

hardest," Grimm said to him in the dugout. "Now you're on your way."

It was expected, too, that the Braves shortly would be on their way, especially once rookie Aaron got going. For though hurt by Thomson's absence, the Milwaukee club was rated a likely contender for the National League pennant, right along with the Dodgers and Giants. As the 1954 Braves took the field, they lined up with Joe Adcock at first, Danny O'Connell at second, Johnny Logan at shortstop and Eddie Mathews at third. The outfield had Andy Pafko and Bill Bruton along with Hank; Del Crandall was the catcher; pitching was strong with Warren Spahn, Lew Burdette, Gene Conley, Bob Buhl, Chet Nichols, Dave Jolly, Ray Crone and Joey Jay.

Their manager, "Jolly Cholly" Grimm, was not only the funniest manager in baseball, but considered one of the finest as well. Grimm had been managing the minor league Milwaukee Brewers when the Braves moved into town and hired him, and though he cracked at the time, "I'm keeping my bags packed, 'cause I don't know how long I'll last around here," it was fairly well understood that the pilot's job would be his for a long time. He had taken a seventh place club and made it a second place pennant contender in his first year, 1953.

During the opening weeks of the 1954 season the Braves floundered in the depths of the second division, finally landing in last place on April 24. This was too much for the usually affable Grimm. That evening he called one of his rare meetings in the clubhouse and blasted the Braves one and all, including Hank, who was hitting about .250.

"I think the trouble with you guys is you're spending too much time looking over the presents everybody gave you last year," the angry pilot rasped. "Now I know I'm supposed to have a joke for every occasion, but this time I'm fresh out. The only joke around here is the kind of baseball you guys have been playing since opening day. And you know something? This keeps up the joke's gonna be on you. There's plenty of time before the June trading deadline you know, and there's plenty of good players in this league would be glad to trade their humpty team for a chance to play in Milwaukee, and don't any of you think you're so good Johnny Quinn wouldn't use you for trade bait."

His usually cheery face stolid, Grimm swept the room with his eyes, then turned and stomped out. The players let out their breaths, looked at each other significantly, then filed out of the stadium, murmuring to each other anxiously. When "Jolly Cholly" got mad, they knew he meant it.

The following night the Braves opened a three-game set at St. Louis against the Cardinals, Spahn facing left-hander Harvey Haddix. In third place, the Cardinals were only one game behind the league-leading Dodgers. It was their misfortune to meet the Braves the day they—and Hank especially—woke up.

Batting third now, behind Bruton and Mathews, Hank got going in the first inning. After Bruton flied out, Mathews doubled. Hank moved up to the plate as unperturbed looking as ever, but inside he was angry at himself. Remembering Grimm's admonitions against pressing, however, he forced his mind and body to relax and wait. He let the first two pitches go by for called strikes. Then, when Haddix curved him a little outside, half wasting the pitch, Hank leaned over and rapped it into center field for a single. Mathews scored and the Braves were in front 1-0.

In the third inning he singled again, beginning a scoring rally; in the sixth a third single knocked Haddix out of the box and brought on relief artist Brooks Lawrence. By now Spahn and the Braves were breezing along 8-2, but Hank was not finished. Batting again in the seventh he hit his fourth straight single and in the ninth he capped his efforts with a terrific blast over the left field wall for his first major league home run. Traditionally, the Braves crowded around him, each making sure to pump his hand energetically in congratulation.

Hank truly felt he had officially arrived on the team.

The rousing 12-3 victory lifted the Braves out of the cellar. Spurred by Hank's explosion and rapidly improving hitting, they began to climb upward. And as they climbed and he continued to hit, Hank found himself more and more the object of the sports writers' attentions. The fans wanted to know more about this twenty-year-old rookie who had come from nowhere apparently to fill—and quite ably—the injured Bobby Thomson's shoes.

Hank's confidence, however, was restricted to his ball playing. He still was young and inexperienced in the social give-and-take among players and sports writers, still unsure of his status, still quite aware of the fact that he was a Negro ballplayer and therefore different. Milwaukee Braves' uniform or no, in the South there was still the business of separate eating and sleeping accommodations in spring training, and though he had not heard any remarks in County Stadium, in other National League cities he did hear an occasional racial catcall from the grandstand—not to mention the ones from enemy dugouts.

So he retreated again into lethargic silence, where it was presumed to be safe, and if sometimes he let slip his mask and indulged in his dry humor, he succeeded more often than not in confusing his listeners, who could not make up their minds whether he was indeed being droll or, instead, was so ignorant and naïve that he was funny. As he had at Eau Claire and Jacksonville, Hank preferred it that way.

Unfortunately, his reticence did not make good copy for the league's sports writers, one of whom cornered him that spring for an interview. "How do you like it up here in the majors?" the writer asked. "Fine," Hank replied.

"You got the looks of a hitter," the writer said.

"I try."

"You find the pitching much different here than in the minors?"

"Ain't been around long enough to find out."

"You mind switching from second base to the outfield?"

"Not if the Skipper don't mind."

The reporter soon gave up, but since copy had to be written on Hank, and perhaps not always to the good, some old Aaron legends from the minor leagues were dusted off, some new stories added that never actually occurred, and the result was a picture of Hank Aaron, Negro rookie, naïve, colorless, funny despite himself, in a Negro minstrel-show kind of way.

Even at the young age of twenty Hank began to realize that he himself, in self defense, had helped foster this impression from his minor league days. Now he didn't like it, but he was neither articulate enough nor secure enough to try to dispel this false image. It would take him years to get rid of it.

Disturbing as these realizations might have been to him in the quiet moments when he had time to think of them, they did not interfere with his playing. He would not let them. Baseball was baseball, and his gratitude at being able to play it for a living was in no way diminished by the inequities that came with being a Negro baseball player. With the bat in his hands he banged out his stature as a professional, and essentially that was all that mattered to him. "What do you look for when you go up there, Hank?" a sports writer asked him in those early days, meaning what kind of pitch, and Hank replied, "The baseball." It was more truth than the dry humor the sports writer missed anyway.

The five-hit day against the Cardinals propelled Hank into the kind of hitting phase Grimm knew he must eventually reach. It was like a cartridge primer setting off the explosive charge that sends a bullet streaking through a rifle barrel. Steadily, Hank pounded away at the National League hurlers, and as he hit, so did the Braves rise out of the depths of the second division, move into the first division, and finally toward the end of May challenge the Dodgers for the league lead.

At home in Milwaukee the Braves took on the Cubs of Chicago. One game behind Brooklyn, they had a Saturday game with the last place Cubs followed by a Sunday doubleheader—a good chance to overtake the Dodgers, who were playing the tough Giants in Brooklyn. But the Cubs declined to be easily obliging. With Bob Rush pitching they went to the bottom of the ninth inning in the Saturday game leading the Braves 2-1.

Leading off the Milwaukeeans last chance was Mathews, who walked. With the tying run on, managerial strategy more often than not in this case would call for a sacrifice bunt, especially with a powerful hitter like Joe Adcock due up after Aaron. But manager Grimm was not particularly an orthodox strategist; he knew moreover that Hank was not an adept bunter—but he did appear to be a good clutch hitter. So he flashed him the "hit away" sign, and Hank hit away, belting Rush's first pitch into the seats for a game-winning homer.

→ In Brooklyn the Dodgers lost, dropping them into a first place tie with the Braves and setting the stage for the Sunday double-header to follow. Though it was too early in the season for any one double-header to be considered crucial, it was even at this stage an important psychological advantage to come out on top at the end of the day's work, aside from the essential, basic fact that many a pennant has been won by one game, and several only after a tie had necessitated a playoff.

So the Braves were primed for this double-header; they wanted badly to win it. In their clubhouse before batting practice they were in high spirits; the locker doors clanged loud and voices were cheerful, but underlying it all was a sharp determination to win both these games against the Cubs. Suiting up in front of his locker Hank felt the tension. At the locker next to his Bruton was lacing his spikes. The speedy center fielder finished knotting his laces and straightened, tapping Hank on the shoulder. "Nothing gets past us today, eh Hank?" he said. "We go in the stands after 'em today."

Hank nodded. "Hope you laced your hitting shoes on today, Billy."

"Got my runnin' ones on," Bruton grinned. "Expect you to be chasin' me around the bases today."

"If I don't it won't be for not trying," Hank said grimly. He finished dressing and followed Bruton through the tunnel under the stands to the Braves' dugout.

77

Grimm called him over at once, showed him the day's line-up that he had just finished preparing. "Hank, you've been a hot man with the bat lately. I'm dropping you into the clean-up spot starting today and moving Adcock up to third. I'm gonna remind you again, don't press. Hittin' fourth ain't that much different than hittin' third."

Hank was not the only one startled by the batting switch. The Braves, the fans and the sports writers were more than a little surprised. True, for the past ten games he had been the club's leading hitter and run producer, but he was still a rookie—a twenty-year-old, comparatively inexperienced rookie at that.

"I think Jolly Cholly finally flipped," one press box veteran exclaimed when the line-up sheets were passed around. "Aaron looks good, but not that good. I don't think the kid can take the pressure, and I wouldn't blame him."

"Well, let's not jump on Charley so fast," another sports writer demurred. "He figures the kid's hot, let's make the most of it. If he don't come through he'll switch again, that's all. Let's see what Aaron does to-day meanwhile."

Grimm was not unaware of the risk he was taking, but as the second sports writer had guessed, the shrewd manager was taking advantage of the fact that Hank was on a hitting spree. In addition, he was counting on the psychology of putting Hank "on the spot" by giving him the responsibility of batting clean-up.

If he analyzed the young rookie correctly, the challenge should bring him "up" for the double-header. Later, Grimm mused, later on was time enough to be concerned. Right now was the opportune time to see whether or not Hank Aaron had the courage to come through.

8...

County Stadium had a festive air about it. The stands were overflowing with noisy fans who had come out on a perfect May Sunday to see their heroes play ball. More than eager to be pleased and entertained, they applauded and cheered every Brave player as he came up for his batting practice swings. The announcement of the line-ups over the public address system occasioned further cheering. In the dugout, manager Grimm grunted at the noise from the grandstand. "We don't win both of these today there's gonna be quite a few thousand disappointed people in Milwaukee tonight," he said loudly.

"Not to mention twenty-five ballplayers and a manager," quipped O'Connell.

"Okay, go get 'em," said Grimm as the plate umpire called "Play ball!" And the Braves ran out of the dugout onto the field.

Bob Buhl started on the mound in the first game, retiring the Cubs in order. Then the Braves quickly opened their attack against Paul Minner. Bruton opened with a single, Mathews flied out, but Adcock

80

walked. Hank, stepping up to the plate for the first time as clean-up hitter for the Braves, looked down at the third base coach to see if there might be a hit-and-run sign on. But he was on his own.

Stretching with two runners on base, Minner came down with a curve low, for a ball. Then a fast ball was low again. Hank looked again at his coach, checking for a "take" sign on the next pitch. Still he was given no orders. He cocked his bat again, and again Minner came down too low, but Hank swung and smashed a low line drive right through the box and into center field for a single. Bruton scored, Adcock went to third and a big rally was on. Three more runs scored before relief pitcher Howie Pollet retired the side. The fans were loudly ecstatic.

The weak Cubs refused to accept defeat readily. Their pitching was terrible but they had several fair hitters on the club, including home run slugger Hank Sauer. They chipped away at Buhl, one run at a time, until a homer by Sauer in the fifth inning tied the score, 4-4. Relief pitcher Ernie Johnson put down the rally. Then, in the bottom half of the fifth, Hank promptly put the Braves ahead again with a line drive homer over the left field fence. A second homer by Sauer, this time with a man on base, gave the Cubs the lead in the eighth inning, 6-5. The game was a thriller, but the fans were not happy.

In the Braves' eighth Mathews led off with a walk. Adcock followed with a single. "C'mon Hank, belt one!" a voice pleaded from the third-base box seats as

Hank walked up to home plate. Pitching carefully to him, Pollet got behind, three balls and a strike. He tried a curve over the inside corner and Hank belted it on a high drive to left center field, dropping between the outfielders. Mathews trotted home with the tying run, Adcock came over with the lead run and Hank slid into third with a triple. He failed to score, but Johnson got the Cubs out in the ninth for a 7-6 victory.

The news from Brooklyn was that the Dodgers had won their game too, keeping the league leadership a tie.

Grimm was immensely pleased with Hank's sensational hitting in the first game, and, though he wouldn't have dared show it or express it aloud, so was Hank. In the stands and in the press box there were few who weren't ready to call the Braves' manager a genius and Hank the greatest thing in the league since Stan Musial.

In the second half of the double-header Warren Hacker of the Cubs opposed Lew Burdette, and this time it was Chicago that jumped into the lead. They picked up two runs in the first inning and another pair in the third to open up a 4-0 margin. On the scoreboard the Dodger game showed them winning again, 3-1. Hacker, meanwhile, was in fine form, fooling the hitters steadily, giving up but one hit through the first four innings.

Then, in the fifth, Pafko pinch-hit for Burdette and singled. The fans began to clap for a rally. "We want a hit!" resounded throughout County Stadium. Bruton obliged with another single. Mathews fouled out, but Adcock doubled, scoring Pafko and putting runners on second and third. Hank—the tying run—dug in next. Cub manager Stan Hack toyed with the idea of walking him intentionally, but decided against it. Walk a kid like Aaron, hot hitter though he may be, with a veteran hurler like Hacker on the mound? It wasn't necessary. He let Hacker pitch, and Hank rapped the first pitch for a tremendous home run. The stands went wild, and on the mound Hacker shook his head ruefully as Hank trotted around the bases.

The score merely was tied, however; the game was still to be won. Into the ninth inning Hacker and relief pitcher Joey Jay battled. The scoreboard showed that the Giants had rallied and beaten the Dodgers. A Braves' victory now would put them on top of the league. But Mathews struck out and Adcock grounded out opening the Braves' ninth, putting it squarely up to Hank again. "How many times can you ask the kid to come through?" Grimm growled to himself from the coaching box.

Hacker coiled in a full windup, threw to the plate good for a strike. The count went to two balls and two strikes; then, taking some speed off a curve, Hacker fooled Hank on the next pitch. But with his quick wrists Hank recovered in mid-swing and still got enough power behind it to send the ball rocketing out to left field along the foul line. It bounced off the wall and ricocheted back to the infield. By the time outfielder Ralph Kiner caught up with the ball Hank was at second with a double. Catcher Crandall, up next, followed with a looping single to left. Hank charged around third, and, though the ball was not hit deep, kept going as Grimm waved him on. He charged desperately down the third base line, realizing that even weak-throwing Kiner would get him out with an accurate relay. He threw himself into a slide, heard the ball plunk into the mitt of big catcher Walker Cooper, kneeling to block the plate. Hank slid around, jabbed his right foot at the plate. Plate umpire Hal Dixon peered into the dust cloud and spread his hands wide. "Safe!" he called—and the Braves moved into first place in the National League.

For a week they rode high, with Hank, batting clean-up, moving his average up to .300, winning ball games spectacularly and dramatically. Chortling to himself for his selection of Hank as clean-up hitter was manager Grimm. "I don't care what he does the rest of the season," the Milwaukee skipper told the sports writers, "Aaron proved to me he has what it takes in the clutch. I put him on the spot, I know I did all right, and if he hadn't come through it would have been more my fault than his, testing him so early. But he did it, and I tell you this kid will be one of the greatest hitters in baseball in a couple years."

Suddenly, however, Hank fell into a slump. The burden of hitting in the most vital spot in the batting order was beginning to tell on him. With just two years of organized baseball behind him he was expected to be the batting leader of a group of recognized stars,

84

and, after a week of playing up to that responsibility, he fell victim to the pressure. As his hitting tailed off, the Braves faltered with him, and soon they found themselves back in second place. Grimm had finally to face the obvious; he shifted Hank back to third in the batting order, and returned Adcock to clean-up.

The removal of the burden helped somewhat, but the Braves began suffering a series of misfortunes. Injuries plagued them. Adcock hurt his hand, Mathews split a finger, then Pafko was operated on for a hernia and Conley wrenched his back. And, of course, Thomson was still sidelined with his broken ankle. When he returned to the line-up in late July Hank was solidly entrenched in the outfield, but was moved to right field to make way for Thomson in left. Pafko the veteran, who had seen fine years with the Cubs and then the Dodgers before being traded to the Braves, was relegated to pinch-hit roles and fill-in assignments in the outfield.

In August the New York Giants put together a winning streak that sent them surging into the league lead, dropping the Braves to third. The race remained a close one through the late summer months and on September 5 the Braves, six-and-a-half games behind, were still in strong contention, until they were hit with their final calamity of the season.

In the first game of a double-header against the Cubs Hank went on a hitting rampage, breaking out of a minor three-day slump. His first time up he doubled, then he homered, then he singled. Finally, in the

85

ninth, he slammed a tremendous drive to left center field. The Braves were far ahead by then 9-2, still Hank ran his hardest. He rounded second and tore into third with a vicious slide. He was safe—but the Braves came running out of the dugout when they saw him lying on the ground, holding his foot, his face twisted in a grimace of pain. He had broken his ankle.

It was ironic, the sports writers wrote the next day, that the same injury to Bobby Thomson that gave Hank his opportunity with the Braves should knock him out of the line-up at such a crucial moment of the pennant race. The doctors said he was lost for the season, and with him went the Braves' last hopes for a pennant. They finished third.

Hank's rookie season was eminently successful. He hit .280, and it was, as one sports writer pointed out, a .280 with a difference. There were .280 hitters who hit .200 against the tough pitchers and the tough teams, fattening up their averages against the weak teams and the weak pitchers. A study of the 1954 record disclosed that Hank's best hitting was against the Dodgers and Giants, and no pitcher in the league could say he fooled Hank consistently.

At the time of his injury Hank had hit thirteen home runs, and was third man on the team in runs batted in, with sixty-nine. He was acclaimed throughout the league as a rookie find, and in the voting for National League Rookie of the Year he lost only by a slender margin to the Cardinals' Wally Moon.

9...

Typical of the early fables that haunted Hank Aaron was that in his lethargic state he was contentedly ignorant of people and events around him. When he was a rookie in spring training for example, he hit a homer off Robin Roberts the first time he faced the famous Phillie hurler. When he returned to the dugout—the legend went—and he was congratulated by his teammates for hitting Roberts so well, he looked at them dumbly and said, "Roberts, who's he?"

It never happened that way at all. Indeed it would have been difficult to understand how a baseball-minded youngster like Hank, watching major league exhibition games raptly when he was eleven years old, could fail to know all about Robin Roberts. Still the fable persisted.

Similarly, when he reported for spring training in 1955 several days before the March 1 date set by Baseball Commissioner Ford Frick, he—and several other early arrivals—was fined fifty dollars by the commissioner. Somehow a legend grew up that Hank had looked puzzledly at the telegram apprising him of the fine, had thrown it away and asked a player, "Who's Ford Frick?"

This too never happened, though Hank did pay the fifty dollars for reporting early. He had, in fact, lost enough of the ingeniousness he understandably had at twenty-one to make sure the Braves paid the fine for him, since it was they, not he, who instigated the idea of reporting earlier than the commissioner allowed. "I'm in fine shape," he had said to general manager Quinn on the phone that winter. "Been working with some kids down here in Mobile, playing basketball and baseball. My legs are fine, my wind's good, I ain't put on any weight . . . " But Quinn was adamant, and Hank reported early.

He was a different Hank than had arrived at spring training the year before, however. Then he had been a minor-league-bound bush leaguer invited to camp for a tryout. Now he was an established outfielder with the Braves, an outstanding sophomore prospect, a respected hitter and fielder and, moreover, a family man with a year-old daughter, Gail Elaine, back in Mobile with his wife Barbara. He was in effect on the road to maturity, off the field as well as on.

That first day of spring training he went out on the field, took his turn in the batting cage and hit the first three pitches over the fence. Stepping out of the cage he flexed his shoulder muscles and said to Del Crandall, the waiting hitter, "Ol' Hank is ready." The Braves themselves were considered ready, too. With virtually the same line-up as the year before, but now with a healthy Bobby Thomson, they were overwhelmingly favored in a nationwide sports writers' poll to win the 1955 pennant.

The Dodgers, however, under manager Walter Alston, opened the season sensationally, winning their first ten games and twenty-two of their first twenty-four. By the time of the All-Star game break, on July 12, the Brooklyn club had a twelve-and-a-half game lead over the Braves, with the Giants in third.

Though the Braves were far from conceding the pennant, there was unmistakably an air of resignation in the locker room. The Dodgers appeared too powerful to overcome, though their veterans, such as Roy Campanella, Pee Wee Reese and Jackie Robinson, were past their prime years. The disappointment was more noticeable in the grandstand, in the newspapers, and in the Braves' front office than it was on the field. The fans turned out in their usual enthusiastic numbers, but here and there were heard a jeer and a grumble. The sports writers too began to throw an occasional barb, and rumors had it that owner Lou Perini and general manager John Quinn were growing restless.

Target for all the criticism was manager Charley Grimm. His easygoing nature, it was felt, was responsible for a lackadaisical manner on the ball club; the players took advantage of him to the point where they were not playing as hard as they could and should have. Some men went so far as to break curfew and

89

training rules and often showed up on the field unfit for play.

Through the entire undercurrent of rumor and criticism Hank rode unaffected. If he was at all aware of the shifting politics within the Braves he didn't show it. Reporters who tried at times to question him about sources of dissatisfaction got a stock answer. "I'm here to play ball. I do it the best I know how. That's all I know and that's all I want to know."

He did indeed know more, as did others on the Braves, but he hardly felt in the position to say anything to a teammate, much less a newspaperman. The worse the internal strife became on the Braves, the more he concentrated on his baseball. As a result he was the team's most consistent hitter in the early part of the season, batting better than .300, and he was named an alternate fielder by National League All-Star manager Leo Durocher. It turned out to be a game-saving choice.

The American League team, led by Al Lopez, the Cleveland Indians' manager, was a heavy favorite to win. They lined up with Mickey Vernon of the Senators at first base, Nellie Fox of the White Sox on second, Chico Carrasquel of the White Sox at shortstop, Jim Finigan of the Red Sox at third, Mickey Mantle of the Yankees in center field, flanked by Ted Williams of the Red Sox in left and Al Kaline of the Tigers in right. Catching was the Yankees' Yogi Berra. Starting pitcher was Billy Pierce of the White Sox.

Against this formidable array the National Leaguers

had Ted Kluszewski of the Reds on first base, Red Schoendienst of the Cardinals on second, Ernie Banks of the Cubs at shortstop, Ed Mathews of the Braves at third; outfielders were Willie Mays of the Giants in center field, Stan Musial of the Cardinals in left, Don Mueller of the Giants in right. With the Dodgers' Roy Campanella out of the game because of an injured hand, the Braves' Del Crandall took over behind the plate. Robin Roberts of the Phillies was starting pitcher.

Hank, who was picked as a replacement for Mueller if he got into the game at all, was especially anxious for a chance since the game was being played in Milwaukee. He chafed on the bench for four-and-a-half innings until Durocher sent him in to run for Mueller in the last half of the fifth inning. By this time the American Leaguers held a strong 4-0 lead, largely on the strength of a three-run homer by Mantle in the first inning. In the sixth inning, when Hank went out to right field, the American League scored once more, for a 5-0 lead.

In the seventh inning he was due to bat fourth, and he hoped that he would get a chance to hit. On the mound now for the American League was the Yankees' Whitey Ford. Mays greeted him with a single. Then Kluszewski and the Cubs' Randy Jackson, who had replaced Mathews at third, flied out to Mantle. That brought up Hank, and Berra trotted out to the mound for a conference with his teammate.

"Any book on this kid?" Ford asked.

91

"They say he hits anything," Berra replied. "Maybe we should try one of each and see if he bites. Nothing too good, though. He's got a lot of power."

Ford nodded and Berra returned behind the plate. Taking his cues from his catcher, Ford pitched carefully to Hank, trying an assortment of curves and different speed pitches, aiming for the corners. Ordinarily Hank would have swung at several that were not too good, but under the circumstances of his first All-Star game he forced himself to wait, and Ford walked him. Angry at himself, Ford let Johnny Logan follow with a single, scoring Mays and sending Hank to third. Pinch hitter Stan Lopata grounded to Carrasquel, who fumbled momentarily, then looked around frantically for a place to throw. Lopata was tearing down the line toward first, not an overly fast runner, but Carrasquel found himself out of position for a throw there. He began to throw home, but saw that Hank was flying like the wind and would beat it; finally he threw to second—wildly. Everybody was safe and Hank was in with the second run. Ford got the next hitter, but now the score was 5-2.

In the eighth inning Ford got the first two batters, then Mays singled. Kluszewski and Jackson singled, scoring Mays, putting runners on first and second. Frank Sullivan of the Red Sox relieved Ford as Hank came up to bat. A little more confident now, with a couple of innings played, Hank reached for an outside curve and hit it safely to right center. Kluszewski scored to make the score 5-4, but Hank wasn't finished on that play. Noticing that Kaline had fielded the ball slowly, he began to run for second; it was a bluff, but he hoped to force Kaline into a hurried throw. True enough the outfielder threw toward second, but it bounced at the edge of the infield and skidded through. Hank then continued on to second and Jackson came all the way around to score the tying run. Sullivan then got Johnny Logan for the final out, but Hank's hit and smart base-running had put the National Leaguers back into the game.

The contest went into extra innings with Sullivan dueling Joe Nuxhall of the Reds. In the twelfth inning the Braves' Gene Conley, losing pitcher of the 1954 All-Star game, redeemed himself, replacing Nuxhall and striking out in order Al Kaline, Mickey Vernon and Al Rosen, three of the American League's leading hitters. Then Musial, first man at bat in the bottom of the twelfth, hit Sullivan's first pitch for a game-winning homer.

In the clubhouse later manager Durocher was high in praise of Hank's part in the victory. "He plays my kind of ball," the colorful manager of the Giants said. "For a kid with his limited experience he plays a heads-up game, and they don't fool with him with pitches, either. You see the way he calmly waited out Ford? That takes moxie. And he hit that single off Sullivan with two strikes on him, so he don't get panicky either. That Aaron's gonna be one of the best in the league, you'll see."

After the All-Star game the Dodgers resumed their

winning ways and romped to the pennant by a thirteen-and-a-half game margin over the Braves. That they didn't fall to third place was in a good measure due to Hank's hitting. He led the team with a .314 average, tying Ted Kluszewski for fifth spot in the league, and led the Braves in runs batted in, with 106. His 27 homers was second on the club only to Ed Mathews' 41, and in doubles he tied teammate Johnny Logan for the league lead with 37. It came as no surprise when the Milwaukee baseball writers voted him The Most Valuable Brave of 1955.

It is axiomatic in baseball that when a club owner makes it a point to give his manager a vote of confidence in public, it's a sure sign that manager is on the spot. So when, at a Milwaukee baseball writers' dinner that winter, Lou Perini spoke out in defense of Charley Grimm, everyone knew it meant that Grimm had better produce a pennant winner in 1956—or else. The air grew noticeably tense as Perini droned on about Grimm, and it took one of Hank's rare moments of wry humor to relax the atmosphere. Going on from Grimm, Perini began to praise Hank's 1955 performance. He talked about his hitting, his fielding, his youth, his alertness, and so forth. Through it all Hank appeared, as usual, to be sleeping. When Perini sat down Hank nudged his neighbor, manager Grimm himself, and said loudly, "Does he mean that about me before I sign my contract or after I sign?"

Perini also announced at that dinner that the Braves

had signed two new coaches for the 1956 season, Johnny Cooney and Fred Haney, further evidence that Grimm was on the spot. Recently resigned as manager of the Pirates, Haney was known as a disciplinarian, a direct contrast to the happy-go-lucky, banjo-playing Jolly Cholly Grimm. Should Grimm falter, everyone knew, Haney was right there to replace him.

And so it turned out. Much as the Braves' players liked Grimm, they couldn't seem to get going for him. On June 16, playing in Brooklyn, they were in fifth place. That morning Grimm announced his resignation and Haney took over the reins.

In all likelihood it was sheer coincidence that the Braves began an eleven-game winning streak the day Haney took over. The men played no harder for Haney than they did for their ex-skipper; if anything the reverse would have been more likely. The players genuinely liked Jolly Cholly, and happy as they were about their winning streak, several Braves expressed regret that it came at a time to make Grimm look bad and Haney look good.

There was evidence that the change helped the team, however. Whether it was Haney or whether any change in managers at that point would have served to jolt the Braves out of their doldrums was a moot point. Jolt the Braves Haney certainly did. There was a lot less horseplay on the field and in the clubhouse. Curfews were strictly enforced and several Braves knew that their record of nightlife carousing meant their days were numbered with Haney in command.

Pre-game meetings became a ritual and on-field strategy was directed from Haney's spot in the dugout. He sat there, implacable, flashing signs to the catcher and the coaches, pulling strings like a puppetmaster. No player stole a base on his own; no player in a tight situation made his own choice of swing away or take.

Many of the players were unhappy with the new order. But the facts were inescapable; with their eleven-game winning streak the Braves had leaped from fifth to first place. The team was playing better all-around ball than they had since first moving to Milwaukee. Hank certainly was having an even better year than his fine one of 1955. Batting in the clean-up position with all the aplomb of a ten-year veteran, he hit at a .350 pace during the Braves' surge. The increasing respect, and sometimes awe, with which veteran stars of the league accorded Hank was made evident on a number of occasions during the summer months of 1956. Manager Haney, a conservative strategist, had ordered more bunts used by the Braves' sluggers. He singled out Hank during the course of a meeting as a notorious non-bunter. "You could add ten points a year to your average if you'd bunt more often," Haney argued. "I want to see you do it more often from now on."

Accordingly, Hank tried it soon afterward. In Ebbets Field one day he noticed that Jackie Robinson, in his last season of a glorious career, was playing him very deep at third base. Here was a chance to do what Haney wants, thought Hank. On the next pitch he tried a bunt, but missed. Yet he noticed, strangely enough, that when he had switched to the bunt position Robinson hadn't made a move to charge in from third. So he tried again on the next pitch, and missed, and again noticed that Robinson failed to charge. With two strikes on him now, Hank swung away and doubled off the left field wall, missing a homer by inches.

After the game, when he had a chance to talk to Robinson, he asked him about the bunt situation. "How come you didn't charge in when you saw me set for a bunt? Especially when I tried it twice? You didn't move up even a foot on me."

The aging Dodger star grinned at him. "Hank, in this small park anytime you want to bunt on me you can have first base. I concede it. I'd rather have you bunt a sure single than hit away here. What did you get today, two doubles off that wall?"

Hank nodded. Haney's wishes notwithstanding, he stopped bunting. To his credit, Haney realized that for Hank to bunt would indeed be a waste, and said no more about it.

For all his conservative manner, Haney was a smart baseball man. He recognized that the unorthodox has its place in the game, too, and he proved his pliability in another dispute concerning Hank's hitting. This one concerned the young outfielder's growing reputation as a "bad-ball hitter," that is, a hitter who swings at pitches not in the strike zone and hits them safely. While theoretically swinging at bad pitches is poor practice, a number of players in history have made an outstanding success at being a bad-ball hitter. When a player is successful at it he is all the more difficult to get out or pitch carefully to; a pitch, for example, that might be thrown deliberately wide or low as a "waste pitch," with a bad-ball hitter is suddenly smacked for a base hit.

It was expected, when Haney took over the Braves, that he might try to tamper with Hank's hitting style, since, as a rather orthodox, conservative manager, it would only be natural for him to frown on bad-ball hitting. Grimm, his predecessor, on the other hand, had delighted in Hank's free-swinging style. Earlier that 1956 season, remarking on it to a reporter, he had laughed. "Hank's strike zone is from the tip of his cap to the tops of his shoes. I haven't seen the likes of as good a bad-ball hitter since Joe Medwick was in his prime," he had added, referring to the ex-St. Louis Cardinal outfielder who many years earlier had been regarded as perhaps the most skillful bad-ball hitter of all time.

Not long after Haney took command he was questioned on Hank's hitting. Considering that the question was asked the morning after Hank had beaten the Cubs with two singles and a home run, it seemed facetious, but the manager understood that it was his own reputation that had prompted the question. He reflected a moment before answering, then said, "Well, I know that Grimm compared Hank with Medwick, and I've heard people say he hits a lot like Shoeless Joe Jackson used to. But I don't want to make any comparisons. As far as I'm concerned Hank is just himself, and, I might add, that's good enough for me. He's relaxed, he's ready, and if he does swing at some bad pitches, well . . . on the other hand, you never have to worry about him passing up a good one, either. All in all, he's about as fine a natural hitter as I've come across."

After talking to Haney, the same Milwaukee sports writer questioned Hank himself about his bad-ball hitting. Hank shrugged. "I make up my mind to swing at a pitch, I swing," he said. "I admit I ain't up there looking for no walks."

It was fortunate for the Braves that during the summer months of 1956 Hank did not look for walks, for his hitting was primarily responsible for the team's continued position at the top of the league. After falling back to second briefly, they were lifted to the top again in a series with the Dodgers when Hank got four straight hits, driving in all three runs in a 3-2 victory. That was on July 14, and it began a twenty-five-game hitting streak that lasted until August 8, when Herman Wehmeier of the Cardinals stopped him. He hit .407 during that streak, and of the fifteen games the Braves won over that period, eight of the victories were directly accounted for by Hank's hitting. Three times a late-inning home run turned the tables in a losing game.

Probably his greatest day during the streak was a Saturday game in Pittsburgh, a slugfest that literally pitted the Pirates against Hank Aaron. He got the

Braves off to a lead in the first inning with a run-scoring single, but the Pirates scored twice in the second inning. In the third Hank tripled with two men on, giving the Braves the lead again, 3-2. In the fifth the Pirates' Dale Long homered, tying the score, but Hank doubled two more runs home in the sixth, making it 5-3. Still the Pirates fought back, countering with a three-run rally in the seventh inning to regain the lead, 6-5. In the eighth inning Hank came up again, with Bruton and Mathews on base, and hit a towering home run that wrapped up the game, 8-6. Even the Pittsburgh fans gave him an ovation as he crossed home plate after the homer; it was one of the most powerful hitting performances ever seen on any baseball field.

In spite of the Braves' position—one-game in the lead over the Dodgers early in August—manager Haney was fuming inwardly. It was no secret that a number of his players were unhappy with his disciplined regime, and, with few exceptions, such as Hank, the men were intolerably casual in their attitude toward the pennant race.

"We should be six, seven games ahead by now," Haney angrily confided to a friendly Milwaukee sports writer. "But those guys are spoiled rotten. They're not giving all they should!"

"Well, you've been riding them pretty close since you took over," the writer challenged, "hasn't it done any good?"

"Sure it's done good," Haney countered. "We're in first place, ain't we? But taking over like I did, after the season has started, there's just so much you can do with a club without risking hurting it. It's different if you take over in spring training, then you can fiddle around and get things going the way you want 'em by the time the season opens. This way . . . " he shook his head in exasperation.

Though the experts had predicted a Braves' pennant in 1956, it was readily apparent that everybody believed in the forecast but the players themselves. It was widely accepted—and those close to the team saw it daily—that up until September the Braves did not feel they had a chance to win the pennant. All through the summer months they displayed no confidence in their league lead, no spirit, no sense of anticipation toward a pennant. It was no surprise, then, that when they woke up early in September and realized for the first time that indeed they did have an excellent chance to win, they fumbled around and didn't know how to clinch it.

The race was a close one, a three-way contest among the Braves, the Dodgers and the Redlegs. Still, as late as Labor Day, Milwaukee held a three-and-one-half game lead over the runner-ups, but in their complacency and with their lack of drive in the clutch, they watched the pennant slowly slip through their fingers. As Haney had said, they could have built a cushiony lead to last them through the final hard days of the pennant race. Instead, on the next to the last day of the season they were a half-game ahead of the Dodgers, with a night game scheduled at St. Louis while the Dodgers took on the Pirates in a double-header. By the time the Braves reported to Busch Stadium to dress, the news was grim: the Dodgers, behind the amazing Sal Maglie and Clem Labine, had beaten the Pirates twice, giving them the league lead by half a game. That meant the Braves had to win their night game or fall a full game behind, guaranteeing the Dodgers a tie for the pennant at least, and the pennant itself should they win their final game of the season.

It was a grim band of Braves that dressed in a hushed locker room. Their backs to the wall now, they were worried and restless. Few of them had expected to get this close to the pennant. Now that the crucial moment was at hand they found their insides twisted into knots. ✓

Hank was quite probably the calmest man in the room. Usually imperturbable anyway, he was one man who knew without thinking about it that he had done his share—and more—in bringing the Braves this far.

Pitching for the Braves in the all-important game was their twenty-game winner, Warren Spahn, against the Cardinals' Wehmeier. As the visiting Braves came up to bat in the first inning, a mighty roar arose from the crowd—many hundreds of rabid Milwaukee fans had made the long journey by bus and train to root for their team in these vital moments. It gave Busch Stadium a World Series atmosphere, and in truth no World Series game ever was filled with more tension and drama.

Bruton opened the game by rifling a single to center.

Adcock flied out, and Mathews fouled out. Hank, the leading hitter not only on the Braves but in the league, stepped in. On the mound Wehmeier racked his memory, tying to recall the magic he had used that August day he had stopped Aaron cold to end his hitting streak. Whatever it was, he knew the chances were he wouldn't fool this hitter with the same assortment of pitches.

The Cardinals' hurler stretched, looked back at Bruton and threw to the plate, outside for a ball. Hank fouled off the next pitch, took another bad pitch for ball two, then fouled off two more. Wehmeier, reaching for a pitch to get him out with, tried a slow curve; it was a bit too low, but Hank golfed it to left center field for a double, scoring Bruton with the lead run. The Milwaukee fans in the grandstand sent up a hoarse cheer. Crandall struck out, ending the brief rally, but the Braves had a 1-0 lead.

Spahn was untouchable. Not a Cardinal got a hit for the first five innings as he preserved his slim lead. In the bottom half of the sixth he retired the first two Cardinals, but then successive doubles simultaneously erased his no-hitter and his lead.

Wehmeier meanwhile settled down effectively, and the game went into extra innings a 1-1 tie. Through the tenth and the eleventh inning the battle continued, the tension building up and the crowd limp from shouting and cheering. The Braves were retired in the twelfth, then, after getting the first batter, Spahn was

103

hit for a double by Stan Musial. Ken Boyer was intentionally walked to set up a double play possibility.

Rip Repulski, the next batter, hit a sharp ground ball right at third baseman Eddie Mathews, and it looked as though the double play strategy had worked. As the Braves and the Milwaukee fans looked on in horror, the ball took a tricky hop and caromed off Mathews' knee into left field. Repulski ran out the hit for a double, and Musial crossed the plate with the winning run. For a stunned moment the Braves stood on the field, rooted to the spot. Then quietly they trooped off to the dugout, defeat registered in the slump of their bodies as they came off the field.

The letdown in the clubhouse was terrible. Spahn sat crying unashamedly in front of his open locker, Hank sat head down, staring unseeing at his hands, wishing he too could find the strength to cry. He felt washed out, empty, exhausted mentally and physically. It would have been better, he thought, to lose the game big, like 12-0, if they were going to lose at all, than lose this way, in extra innings, on a bad hop grounder. He, as did the rest of the Braves, had no illusions about the pennant now. Technically they were still in the race; a win tomorrow coupled with a Dodger loss would mean a tie and playoff. But the gloom in the clubhouse accurately reflected their hopes at gaining a tie. They did what they had to do the next day, beating the Cardinals in the season's finale, but the Dodgers won their game with the Pirates, capturing the pennant by one game.

When the figures were all in, Hank came out the winner of the National League batting crown with a .328 average. At 22, he was the second youngest man ever to win the batting title; the youngest, Pete Reiser, was one month and fourteen days younger than Hank when he won the title in 1941, playing for the Dodgers.

In the 1956 season Hank was the only major league player to get two hundred hits, and he led the league in doubles with 34, but everyone on the Braves knew he would have traded all his hits for one that could have won that vital night game in St. Louis.

When the Braves returned to Milwaukee after their final game in St. Louis they had one great desire in common: to pack their personal belongings at County Stadium and get out of town fast. After the many Milwaukee newspaper stories accusing them of choking up under pressure and blowing a sure pennant, they expected nothing but a cold shoulder from the normally enthusiastic city. On the plane ride back from St. Louis they stared silently out the ports, each man hoping he could get away as quickly as possible, meeting as few people as possible, once the plane landed. As they circled over Billy Mitchell Field and banked for a landing, the players could see a huge crowd gathered below. With some justification, they looked at each other worriedly.

"Anybody see any tar and feathers?" cracked Joe Adcock, trying to ease the strain.

"Hope they got plenty of cops down there, that mob

must be ready to run us out of town on a rail," muttered Lew Burdette. Certainly every man on the team felt the crowd was there to hoot and jeer.

Del Crandall walked through the door first when the landing ramp was pushed in position. Burdette followed, then Spahn, Adcock and Hank. They stood on the ramp platform, hesitating before descending the steps. The crowd surged forward, thousands of people, men, women and children—even women with children in their arms. They broke through the thin lines of police, surrounding the plane. The hesitant players at the top of the stairs began to make out the words that were being shouted and saw the tears in the eyes of those in front of the crowd. The shouts were words of sympathy and encouragement; the tears were of regret and understanding, not anger.

With a lump in his throat Hank walked down the stairs with his teammates, was pummeled on the back and had his hand shaken with the rest of them as the players made their way slowly through the crowd to the bus that would take them into town. "God bless you Hank!" he heard one woman say, and, "You did your best, Hank!" a man in a business suit said to him, patting him on the back.

Funny how it often takes misfortune to bring out the best in people, he thought, as he settled down peacefully in his seat on the bus. In less than a minute he heard Billy Bruton's voice say, dimly, "There's goes ol' Hank, asleep again." And he smiled.

10...

It can be said with much justification that the 1957 season began for the Braves a moment after the 1956 season ended. After beating the Cardinals in the meaningless final game of the 1956 season, the Braves filed silently into the clubhouse for the usual post-mortem meeting with the manager. But if they had been expecting anything like the typical pat-on-the-back, wait-till-next-year platitudes they were quickly advised of their error. Tough Fred Haney had other ideas.

He stomped into the dressing room, his eyes hard, his jaw set grimly. He stood for a moment in the midst of the half-dressed men, his eyes flicking deliberately from man to man, and those who knew that they had failed their fellow players cringed inwardly under that scathing glance. Almost in a whisper, Haney told them that he had a few words to say to them in parting. Just a few words; short, but maybe not so sweet.

"A lot of you fellas had a good time this season. A real good time. And I want to tell all of you to have a good time over the winter. Enjoy yourselves. Because when you report back for spring training you're going to work like you never worked before. And if you think I was mean this year, next year you're going to find me the worst so-and-so you ever met in your life."

The men found him true to his word when they met again in Florida five months later. Haney greeted his players in spring training the way he had parted from them. "I want to get something straight from the very beginning," he said. "I don't care what you think about me or say about me. I just want to make you guys better ball players. By the time this season is over I guarantee you'll hate my guts, but you'll be spending your World Series checks by then so it won't matter."

No club ever worked harder in spring training. They drilled from ten-thirty in the morning to four-thirty in the afternoon. Haney even had them running in the rain. Only a tropical shower forced them indoors, and then the manager and his coaches drilled them in signs and strategy and enemy pitchers and hitters. For hours on end Haney had them practicing slides until big "strawberry" bruises appeared on their legs, puffed up and swollen.

Haney spared no one, rookie or veteran. In truth there probably was not a man on the Braves who at some time the season before, had not committed some bush league blunder. Even Hank once had been guilty of trying to score standing up instead of sliding and had been tagged out. So every player drilled in fundamentals—leading off bases, making run-downs, working cut-off plays, practicing double steals and hit-and-run.

The players did not complain. They did not even

appear to be hostile. They all knew—as did Haney, the Milwaukee sports writers and the fans—that underneath there was a flicker of rebellion, of wait-and-see. The word was that unless Haney's tough tactics paid off fast when the season opened there was danger of open rebellion against the manager; a Braves team had done it before, in 1949 against Billy Southworth, in Boston.

It didn't take long to dissipate the rebellion talk. The Braves jumped into the 1957 pennant race under a full head of steam, winning their first five games and nine of their first ten. The season was barely two weeks gone before everybody was asking: "Who's going to stop the Braves?"

Winning was only half the story; it was how they were winning that really told the tale. It was hard to believe that this aggressive, high-spirited ball club was the exact same aggregation that had blithely plunged itself into disaster the year before. They had the same faces, the same uniforms with the same numbers, but five of their first nine victories were by one-run margins, four times they had to come from behind in the late innings to win—precisely the kind of game they were losing in 1956. They were playing heads-up, confident ball, hanging on, taking advantage of the breaks, never giving up until the final out.

They lined up again with Joe Adcock on first, Danny O'Connell on second, Johnny Logan at shortstop, Ed Mathews on third; Bill Bruton was in center field, Bobby Thomson in right, Hank in left; Del Crandall

109

was behind the plate; pitchers were Spahn, Burdette, Buhl, Conley, Crone, Bob Murff, Ernie Johnson and Taylor Phillips.

Haney readily acknowledged the change in his team. "The difference is that last year hardly any of them figured they had a chance at the pennant. This year there isn't one of them that doesn't believe we will win, and they're playing as though every game was the pennant clincher."

Even Hank seemed spurred to greater heights of performance. In the early weeks his hitting supplied the bulk of the Braves' power, providing the margin in many of their victories. The first home run he hit meant the difference in a 2-1 win over the Reds in Milwaukee's opening streak. The next day his bases-loaded single in the tenth beat the Giants. A week later, after his ninth-inning, three-run homer sent a game with the Pirates into extra innings, he added the game-breaker with a triple in the eleventh inning, scoring the winning run on a fly ball.

Despite their winning splurge in the first two weeks the Braves were not running away from the rest of the league. The Dodgers, Cardinals and Redlegs remained in hot pursuit. Through the spring months the first division of the National League was like a treadmill, each team running as hard as it could, passing others at times and being passed, but nobody apparently making any real headway. The margins between the four clubs were so close that losing one game often meant a two-place drop in the standings; a round of

110

Sunday double-headers could scramble the whole division by nightfall.

No matter what the standings, a great many sports writers, baseball experts and fans privately conceded the pennant to the Braves after June 15. On that day Milwaukee obtained second baseman Red Schoendienst from the Giants in trade for pitcher Ray Crone, outfielder Bobby Thomson, and second baseman Danny O'Connell. A thirty-four-year-old veteran who had been a star with the St. Louis Cardinals before going to the Giants, Schoendienst had been an All-Star second baseman eight times. Generally regarded as the finest fielding second baseman in the league and a tough hitter in the clutch, he was now, with the Dodgers' Jackie Robinson retired, the best all-around second baseman in the league, if not all baseball.

The day Schoendienst arrived on the Braves it was obvious that this was the one missing link needed to jell the ball club. He took charge of the infield, molded it into a smoothly efficient unit, and became, without anyone saying it, the leader of the entire team.

The Braves were in fourth place when Schoendienst took over. A week later they were in second, and Hank was in the middle of a fifteen-game hitting streak. At the All-Star break—and he was named to the outfield for the third straight year—Hank was leading the league's hitters in everything: average, with .350, hits, homers, runs batted in and total bases. He was the scourge of National League pitching.

The regard in which he was held throughout the

league was typified in a game against the Pittsburgh Pirates right after the All-Star game. In a double-header against the same team a week earlier he had gotten six hits, including two homers, personally accounting for the winning runs in both games. Now, as he came to bat in the first inning, Pirate manager Bobby Bragan signaled from the bench to his catcher Dick Rand to call for a knuckle ball. Rand blinked in astonishment. The situation didn't seem to call for a knuckle ball; it was a peculiar, erratic type of serve that pitcher Vernon Law preferred to save for a particular, tight situation. Here it was the first inning and nobody was on base. He hesitated, but Bragan flashed the sign again, and Rand relayed the order to the mound.

In the dugout Bragan explained to one of his puzzled coaches. "Let's see what Aaron can do with a knuckler to start the day with."

On the mound, puzzled Law finally accepted his catcher's sign and threw a knuckle ball. Hank blasted it out of the park for a home run.

In the dugout Bragan threw up his hands in resignation. "I give up. No matter what you throw, this guy'll hit it!"

When pitcher Ray Crone reported to the Giants he was immediately badgered by the Giant hurlers, who figured that as an ex-teammate of Hank's, Crone might have some tips for them.

"How can you pitch to Aaron?" Johnny Antonelli asked.

"Not good," Crone shook his head.

"But he must have a weakness," Curt Barclay said.

"If he has," Crone said, "nobody's found it yet."

Shortly afterward Hank earned a testimonial from Roy Campanella, the Dodger catcher and one of the all-time greats both with the bat and the catching tools. Between games of a double-header, after Hank had demolished the Dodgers in the opener with three straight doubles, Campanella was talking to a group of Milwaukee and New York sports writers in the Dodger dugout.

"You can't fool that boy Aaron on anything," the Dodger catcher said. "No matter what pitch you call for on him or where you call it he gets his bat on it with power. I've seen him guess wrong on a pitch and still manage to pull it into the stands. In my time in this league he's the best right-handed hitter I've ever seen. And Henry's still a boy."

If further evidence were needed on Hank's stature as a hitter, it was given by manager Haney himself during the young outfielder's fifteen-game streak. In one game Hank came to bat with runners on first and second and two out. The pitcher got behind, three balls and no strikes. The natural, orthodox move is to let the batter take the next pitch, the "automatic strike." It was the thing Haney would order ninety-nine times out of a hundred—but apparently not when Hank was the batter, for he flashed the "hit" sign, and Hank promptly sent a fast ball flying out of the ball park.

The next time the situation arose Haney did the

same thing, but to his consternation Hank let the pitch go by for a strike. The fact that two pitches later he singled didn't make Haney much happier about his ignoring the sign. After the game Haney talked to him about it. "What was wrong with that three-and-oh pitch?" he asked. "Didn't you see me flash the hit sign?"

Hank hesitated. His initial reaction was to lapse into the minstrel-man Hank Aaron of old, to try to make a joke out of it or even better, play dumb. Last year he would have gone deadpan and said something like, "Hit sign? I thought that was the take sign." He couldn't do that now. He was only twenty-three, but he had proved a lot of things in his seasons with the Braves, things that he felt would make it a shame if he hesitated or retreated now, things that made it imperative that he say what he wanted to say. Forcing on himself a confidence he did not quite feel, he said to Haney. "I tell you Skipper, he took a little speed off that pitch. When I'm hitting three-and-oh, I like a little something extra on it, not off."

Haney actually had not expected any answer in particular, but this one threw him off stride. He knew Hank's reputation as a rather amiable fellow who, stories went, sometimes forgot what inning it was or who was pitching. He was taken aback, therefore, on two counts: one, Hank was supposed not to reason about such things; two, he had never before expressed the right to out-guess the manager. Outstanding ball players are sometimes given that privilege by their managers, but had this been anyone but Hank, Haney would not have let it pass. He knew, however, that this moment contained no overtones of rebellious disobedience by a ball player. Hank had not been among the unhappy element on the Braves when he had applied the whip. Haney realized that Hank was simply exercising the privilege of a few great hitters to think for themselves and on occasion ignore a manager's orders. Also, the Braves' manager knew, without further discusion, that Hank was aware of the fact that even the greatest hitter could exercise that judgment on rare occasion only—and get away with it. Right or wrong, the manager was the manager.

As it was, instead of berating Hank, Haney saw fit to praise him publicly the next day. Ordinarily not given to superlatives, Haney—for Haney—was practically raving. "In the next couple of years they'll be talking about Hank the way they do about Hornsby," he said, referring to Rogers Hornsby, a Hall-of-Famer regarded as one of the greatest hitters in baseball history. "Hornsby's best power was to right center field," Haney continued. "This kid's got just as much there and more to the other fields. He's one of those things that come along once in a lifetime for a manager."

"Would you compare him to Ty Cobb?" asked a listener, mentioning another of the all-time greats of baseball.

"Certainly," Haney replied, "as a great hitter. But Cobb was the only great one I can recall who was nervous at the plate. The real good hitters are always

115

relaxed. Hank—he's as loose as a can of worms, the most nonchalant hitter I've ever seen."

In July disaster appeared to strike the Braves despite their heroic efforts. This time it was injuries that threatened to undo all of Haney's hard work. Joe Adcock broke his leg, and young Frank Torre took his place. Shortstop Johnny Logan was hurt next, and Felix Mantilla replaced him. Then Bill Bruton crashed into Mantilla as they converged on a pop fly, hurt his knee and was lost for the season. This necessitated an outfield shift. Hank moved into center, and Bob Hazle was brought up from Wichita to share duties with Andy Pafko in left field. Wes Covington, who had been brought up earlier from Wichita to replace the traded Bobby Thomson, remained in right. When Pafko was injured, catcher Crandall was pressed into service as a left fielder, with Del Rice and Carl Sawatski taking turns catching.

Haney now began to see fade the team he had worked so hard to build in spring training. Instead of the same faces, the same uniforms but a new-spirited version of the 1956 club, he now had a team that looked like this: Frank Torre at first base, Red Schoendienst at second, Felix Mantilla at shortstop, Ed Mathews at third. Covington, Hank and Hazle in the outfield, Crandall catching, and the same group of pitchers. Except for the pitchers, only Hank, Mathews and Crandall were 1956 regulars.

If ever in that season the Braves would fall apart, this was the spot, with much more valid excuse than they had the previous year. But having been set an example by the regulars, the replacements caught the fire and played hard, smart baseball. Just as the team began to work again smoothly, disaster struck again. This time it looked like the proverbial straw that would break the Braves' back.

They were in Philadelphia holding a slim, half-game lead over the second place Cardinals, with three games scheduled against the fifth place Phillies—who were only five games behind the league leaders, it was so close a pennant race. The score was 3-0 in the Phillies' favor when Hank came up in the seventh inning and hit a tremendous drive to right center field. From second base Schoendienst romped home to score easily, and Hank tore around the basepaths, trying for a triple. As third baseman Woody Smith set himself for the relay, Hank slid hard into third, ahead of the tag, but the Braves on the bench heard him yelp as he jammed his foot full speed into the bag. He sat up quickly, but when he tried to push himself erect his left ankle gave way under him and he fell back on the base.

In the dugout Haney threw his hands over his face. "Oh no! Not him!" he cried. Then he jumped up and hurried over to where the trainer and the Braves' players had gathered around the injured man. Haney elbowed his way through the knot of players to Hank's side. The trainer was kneeling, feeling and looking at Hank's ankle. He looked up at the manager. "Let's help him off the field. He's through for today."

117

In the clubhouse the trainer continued his examination. Haney left the day's managing to one of his coaches and stood glued next to the rubbing table where Hank lay. "How bad is it, Doc?" Hank asked, frowning in pain as the trainer pressed probing fingers into the flesh around his ankle.

"Can't say yet. It don't look like a break. Probably just a bad sprain. We'll take you into town for x-rays right away though. Don't pay to take chances."

The x-rays turned up no break, fortunately, but Hank did have badly sprained tendons. "How long you think I'll be out?" he asked the team's regular physician.

"Can't say, depends on how you come around," came the doctor's reply. "Sprained ankles are strange things. They heal peculiarly. But in this case I'd hazard a guess that you'll be unable to play ball for two weeks."

"Two weeks!" Hank cried.

"Two weeks!" Haney echoed him. "We can't lose him for two weeks. It'll kill us!"

The doctor shrugged. "If he tries to come back too soon and injures that ankle before it heals right, you can forget about him for the rest of the season. If the boy's lucky and he heals especially fast, then maybe ten days. But that's about the minimum. I suggest he go home and rest so neither of you are tempted by seeing him around in uniform."

Haney groaned, but he had no choice. Hank, too, realized that it would be foolhardy to ignore the doctor's warning. He hobbled back to Mobile on a cane, therefore, and decided to use this time off to good advantage. For some time he had been urged by a Milwaukee brewery to accept an off-season job as a representative. "Buy a house, settle down in Milwaukee," the head of the firm had told him.

Long discussions with his wife had decided them in favor of the idea, and in the few idle moments he found when the team was at home, he had quietly looked at some houses offered him by real estate agents. Now, with his ankle injury sidelining him, was a fine time, he thought, to settle on a house, buy it, and move the family to Milwaukee. He certainly needed the room; the Aarons were now four, with a son, Henry Jr., added to the family the previous February and his wife expecting again in December.

In Mobile he and his wife had a long, final talk about the house they liked the best. Hank had a picture of it, supplied by the agent, and they sat and stared at the photo in silence a long moment. The house was what they wanted, no doubt of it. But it was in a white neighborhood. Would they be welcomed there? they wondered. Would there be serious repercussions? His wife balked at this possibility, but Hank was less worried.

"I'm not kidding myself, Barbara, nor you either," he said. "I don't think the average colored person could live there. But I feel sure those people will accept us because of who I am."

"You mean because you're Henry Aaron, the baseball player?"

"That's exactly right. Being with the Braves may not make me any different as a person, but it gives me a certain kind of privilege I wouldn't have otherwise, and I think we should take advantage of that."

"But in a way, it's not right, is it?" she said. "I mean, knowing they don't really accept you for what you are, but only for what you are in a baseball uniform."

"Don't I know that?" he countered. "But you're asking for something you just won't get and I think we should take advantage of a fine opportunity without looking into all the why's and wherefore's. Besides, it may start out that those people are accepting the baseball player and his family, and then after a while they'll just like us, period."

"And if they don't?"

He shrugged. "As long as they let us live there peacefully. Look honey, maybe they just accept me as a baseball player, but I accept them as human beings. All I want is what most people want—a decent place for my wife and kids. It doesn't make no difference if people don't want to talk to me."

They bought the house and moved in that summer. Hank thought it would be best to move in quickly while he still hobbled and could therefore be around the house for the first few days. Hoping for the best and, for all his uttered words of bravado, fearing the worst, he made himself conspicuous, feeling out the reactions of his neighbors. As any new home owner would he made trips to the hardware store and the supermarket, the bakery and the butcher shop, putting in food, buying an extra hammer and some nails, a small can of paint for touching up, little things his wife found she needed after moving in.

As he made the rounds of the shops and walked around the neighborhood he could have cried with joy at the reception he was accorded. There were the coolly polite ones, of course, and perhaps one or two inwardly hostile, but there was no doubting that on the whole he and his family were made welcome in their Milwaukee home. Instead of trouble he was met with handshakes and good wishes for a speedy recovery, and the neighborhood youngsters crowded around him on the street begging for his autograph and advice. "How should I hold the bat, Hank?" "How do you hit the curves, Henry?" they badgered him, some calling him Hank and some calling him Henry, but all eager and grinning and anxious to be his friend.

He tried to find time for all of them, until one of his new neighbors was prompted to remark, "I don't know how he stands it, all those kids bothering him. He's got more patience than any man I've seen."

Hank was pleased with his choice. "These are real nice, warm, friendly folks," he told a Milwaukee sports writer several days after moving in. "I couldn't have picked a nicer place to live."

He still wasn't kidding himself. He knew his acceptance was as Hank Aaron, star of the Braves, and that he should not expect to live there on the same terms as white people could. But he hadn't bargained for any

121

BLAIRSVILLE SENIOR HIGH SCHOOL
BLAIRSVILLE, PENNA.

more than that when he bought the house. He was well satisfied.

Now what irked him was his injured ankle. For a few days the excitement of moving and the new neighborhood had helped him forget. That was over now, and he knew he had to get back in shape to play. If he needed any extra prompting it was provided for him one morning as he limped down to the store to buy a newspaper. The Braves had played in New York the night before, and he didn't get to hear the score on the late news broadcasts. Outside the store he met one of his neighbor's youngsters. The boy looked at him gravely and said, "Hank, when is your foot gonna be all better. We need you!"

Hank smiled. "Soon, soon," he said, patting the boy's head. He walked inside and bought a paper, turned first to the sports pages. The Braves had lost again.

He guessed maybe they did need him at that. He tucked the paper under his arm. Grimly, he limped home.

11...

Two days later, when the Braves returned for a long home stand, a worried Fred Haney walked into the County Stadium dressing room and found Hank on the rubbing table having his ankle taped by the trainer. Haney blinked at him, calculating rapidly in his mind. "It's only eight days since you got hurt, what are you doing here?" he rasped.

Hank grinned at him. "Ol' Hank is ready," he said.

Haney snorted. "Maybe you are and maybe you ain't. We'll see about that. When you get your spikes on come on out and we'll see how you run." He turned and stalked out of the room, secretly pleased at Hank's determination. He dared to hope that his best hitter could indeed return to action sooner than the doctor had predicted. The Braves were in second place now, a game behind the Cardinals, only a game and a half ahead of the third place Dodgers, and in fact only five games ahead of the fifth place Phillies. With Hank out of the line-up they were in danger of falling into the second division.

Ten minutes later the outfielder walked out on the

123

BLAIRSVILLE SENIOR HIGH SCHOOL
BLAIRSVILLE, PENNA.

field, his left leg a little stiff, but he wasn't limping too badly. Haney studied his face as he walked, watching for a telltale wince. He was gratified not to notice any, but he had a hunch why.

"The doc shoot you full of Novocain?" he asked when Hank reached him near the batting cage.

Hank nodded, smiling.

Haney grunted. "You do any running before today?"

"I played some catch with the kids in the neighborhood."

"That's a big help. Well, run around the field a couple of times. See how it feels. If it's okay, take outfield and hitting practice. See if it can hold up when you have to put pressure on it."

Hank loped out along the base line and began to circle the field in a slow trot, hoping the Novocain and the tape would do their job. He was stiff and awkward at first, but he felt no pain, and though he ran favoring his left leg he thought it would hold up well enough in a game. He trotted past the batting cage, nodded at Haney that he was okay, then ran out to the outfield to catch fungoes hit by the coaches. Here, putting extra pressure on the ankle by starting and stopping quickly, he felt twinges of pain, but he ignored it. The only thing he cared about was the ability to cover ground; pain he could stand. After fifteen minutes of catching fly balls he was in a sweat from his exertions. He came in off the field, toweled his face and hands in the dugout, picked a bat out of the rack and took his place in the batting cage. Here was the real test. He hit off his

124

front foot, the left one. If his ankle held up now he would be all right.

Haney stood behind the cage, watching him narrowly. The wily manager wasn't fooled by Hank's poker face. He had been around baseball too long not to know as much about ankle injuries as the trainers. He knew that even with Novocain Hank was hurting. But he needed the young man in the line-up; if he could play and stand the pain, he would play.

Anxiously Haney looked on. Hank swung gingerly at the first few pitches, testing his ankle and his timing, after the eight-day layoff. Then, satisfied that the ankle would not collapse under the strain, he began to hit naturally. Three times in a row he caromed a ball off the left field wall, then he sent a towering shot into the bull pen, more than four-hundred feet away. He turned and looked at Haney, and nodded. Haney nodded in return, walked back to the dugout and began penciling in a line-up for the day's game against the Dodgers. In the number four spot he wrote in Aaron.

A great roar went up in County Stadium when the public address system announced Hank's name batting fourth. The fans stood up by the thousands, whistling and cheering, calling his name, and their applause echoed in the great expanses of the grandstands when he ran out to take his position in center field. Covington and Hazle shook his hand, welcoming him back, then Warren Spahn wound up and threw the first pitch of the ball game.

The contest was a see-sawing slugfest, with both Spahn and Dodger starter Johnny Podres knocked out of the box by the fourth inning. With Hank contributing a run-producing single in the first inning on his first at bat after his injury, the Braves had a 6-5 lead after six innings. The Dodgers got the tying run off reliever Ernie Johnson in the seventh inning and added two more in the ninth to gain the lead.

As the Braves came up to bat in their half of the ninth, Haney called on Pafko to hit for the first batter, Johnson. The veteran came through with a single, but Schoendienst popped up and Logan was struck out by Dodger relief ace Clem Labine. Haney fidgeted in the dugout. He was well aware of the psychological importance in winning this game. The players were depending on Hank to pull them back into the lead; if they lost this game, with him back in action, they might count themselves out of the race again.

It was up to Mathews now to keep the game alive. Hank kneeled in the on-deck circle, waiting. Mathews came through with a double, Pafko holding at third. The tying runs were on base now; Hank was the winning one.

Labine, with his great curve, went to work carefully. Hank fouled off the first pitch, passed up the next two bad ones. He swung and missed at a curve, for strike two. The crowd screamed for a hit. Haney stood in front of the dugout, one foot up on the steps, watching, knowing that after the seventh inning Hank had asked trainer Bob Feron for another shot of Novocain.

The two-two pitch came down and Hank swung. The sound of the bat meeting ball was loud and sharp. The ball took off on a rising line, zoomed over outfielder Gino Cimoli's head and was still going strong when it crashed into the stands for a game-winning homer.

The clubhouse later was full of grins. Even the hissing of the showers seemed to have a merrier sound. On the rubbing table Hank was having his foot examined by Feron, surrounded by the sports writers. The trainer, ignoring them, heaved a loud sigh and shook his head. "No damage. But leave the tape on for a while. If I cut it off now that foot'll swell up like a balloon. First thing tomorrow morning I'll cut it off and put new tape on."

The sports writers were impatient. "You feel much pain during the game, Hank?" one asked.

"Some," Hank said. "Wasn't too bad."

"What kind of pitch did you hit for the homer?" came the usual question.

"A curve."

"Were you figuring he'd throw you the curve in that spot?"

Hank shook his head. "I don't guess when I got two strikes on me. The only thing I look for then is the baseball. If it's there, I hit it."

Haney marched in and broke up the questioning. "He's had a tough day fellas," he told the writers. "Let him get home and rest. We got a twi-night double-

127

header tomorrow and I figure we need him to help us win both of them."

The prediction was accurate. At times limping noticeably, nevertheless, Hank assaulted Dodger pitching the next evening with a savagery that had the Milwaukee fans screaming with delight. In the opener he knocked Don Newcombe from the pitcher's box with a three-run homer, then hit relief pitcher Ed Roebuck for a two-run double, the Braves winning, 9-5. In the second game Don Drysdale was the victim. The young right-hander of the Dodgers had a 3-1 game wrapped up until the eighth inning. Then, his control slipping, he walked Schoendienst and Mathews. Hank smacked his first curve for a double, tying the score, and scored the winning run a moment later on Covington's single.

Suddenly the whole pennant race cracked wide open. Led by Hank's exciting hitting—his ankle was healed completely in a few days—the Braves won ten straight games. Simultaneously all the other pennant contenders seemed to fall apart. The Cardinals lost ten of eleven, the Dodgers eight of twelve, the Reds seven of eleven and the Phillies six of nine. It was as though Hank's return to action was the signal for the rest of the league to surrender. A game behind in second place when he came back, they found themselves twelve days later eight-and-a-half games ahead of the Dodgers and Cardinals, ten games ahead of the Reds and eleven-and-a-half ahead of the Phillies. Never had rival clubs cooperated so perfectly with a pennant challenger. From a tight, five-team race it became a run-away.

It wasn't all smooth sailing, however. Through the remaining days of August they kept up the pace and their lead, but nobody dared mention the pennant—not yet. Even the Milwaukee papers mentioned the subject cautiously, when they mentioned it all. The fans kept their fingers crossed, looked at each other meaningfully, but said nothing, afraid of jinxing their team.

On September 2 the Braves went wild in a 23-10 win over the Cubs, Hank sending home six runs with a double and two singles. The next day he helped Spahn to his eighteenth victory of the year and record-breaking forty-first shutout of his career, banging a homer and two singles in an 8-0 victory.

Then the Braves' machine began to sputter. They lost three straight. Spahn halted the skid momentarily, but they dropped three more in a row, won two, then lost two more. Their lead on September 15 was cut to two-and-a-half games over the Cardinals. Even Hank fell into a mild slump during those eleven games, losing seven points off his batting average and hitting but one homer, though that one, his fortieth of the season, pulled a 4-3 victory out in the ninth inning of one game.

The Cardinals were applying the pressure now, waiting for the Braves to crack as they did the year before in the final stages of a tight pennant race. But this time they didn't panic. With Haney goading them on and the spectre of last year's debacle hanging over them, they didn't give up. They refused to resign themselves to another runner-up finish. They went out on the field every day and played their hearts out, win or lose, and, as it must happen when a team plays that kind of baseball, the tide finally turned in their favor.

Out of contention by this time, the Brooklyn Dodgers gave them a hand, stopping a Cardinal streak with a 6-1 victory while the Braves were beating the Giants. That extended the Milwaukee lead to four games, with only nine left to play. But the Cardinals weren't giving up either. They beat the Dodgers in extra innings the next day, while the Braves lost.

Finally, dramatically, the Cardinals found themselves in Milwaukee for what would of necessity be the deciding series. There were four games left to play, and the Braves held a four-game lead. One more Milwaukee victory and the pennant would fly over County Stadium.

Of course there was barely a foot of standing room in the grandstand that night, much less a seat to be had. Fans flocked from hundreds of miles around to squeeze into County Stadium, hoping to see a game they could tell their grandchildren about in years to come—the game that gave Milwaukee its first pennant. From the moment the Braves came on field to take their batting practice the din in the stadium was terrific.

Lew Burdette started for the Braves, against the Cardinals' Larry Jackson. The Red Birds scored first, tallying two runs off Burdette on a bases-loaded double by Musial in the third inning. While the anxious crowd yelled for the Braves to start a rally, Jackson kept them in check, yielding just three hits for the first six innings. Then Logan singled to start the Braves seventh. The fans began clapping rhythmically, chanting, "We want a hit! We want a hit!" A groan went up as Mathews lined out to left field.

Hank stepped in to hit, and the clapping and chanting began again. Jackson stretched, tried a curve outside, for a ball. Another curve was good for a strike. Expressionless, Hank waited at the plate. Again Jackson went into a stretch, peeked over his shoulder at Logan, delivered to the plate. Hank swung, cracked the ball sharply to right center field for a hit. Logan circled the bases and came around to score the Braves' first run as Hank slid into second safely for a double. The fans were hysterical, then went even wilder when Torre followed with a single. Racing around the bases as though pursued by fiends, Hank churned up the turf heading for home. The throw from right fielder Del Ennis was fast and true. Catcher Hal Smith took it, kneeling to block the plate. Hank slid in hard, upset the burly catcher, and the plate umpire spread his hands in the "safe" sign. The game was tied.

The score remained 2-2 through the eighth, and then through the ninth as the game went into extra innings. The tension was becoming unbearable. Every pitch, every swing brought a shout from the crowd. In the bottom of the tenth the Braves threatened, and Haney was forced to pinch hit for Burdette, though he had

131

been pitching a great game. The pinch hitter failed, and Don McMahon came on to pitch to the Cardinals in the eleventh. The young relief artist sent the Cardinals down without a murmur, earning a cheer from the fans. In the bottom of the eleventh the Braves had the top of the batting order coming up. The crowd began to stomp and chant once again.

Schoendienst led off with a walk, Logan, trying to sacrifice him to second, bunted into a force play. Mathews fouled out. That put it once more up to Hank. The stamping of feet and the clapping of hands was deafening. All over the ball park fans stood up in groups and screamed at Hank to get a hit. He stood there at the plate, stolid and unmoving, bat cocked. Jackson delivered, Hank swung—and County Stadium went crazy. There was no doubt about where the ball was going from the split second it left the bat with a resounding crack. The sphere flew in a white blur out toward left field. Wally Moon, the Red Bird fielder, ran several steps backward, then turned and watched futiley as the ball soared into the grandstand, a home run that won the game and the first pennant in Milwaukee Braves' history.

The stadium was in an uproar. As Hank loped swiftly around the bases, suppressing a grin, special police quickly lined up along the base lines. Already frantic fans were spilling over the railings of the box seats, bent on reaching the players. Schoendienst crossed home plate, stepping on it hard, then turned and waited for Hank along with every other member of the Braves. The instant he touched home Hank was mobbed by his teammates. They jumped on his back and pummeled him, dragged and carried him away, finally lifting him on their shoulders and bearing him triumphantly back to the dugout.

County Stadium meanwhile was insane. Strangers hugged and kissed each other. Programs, paper cups, cushions, hats, all manner of debris filled the air and rained down on the playing field. The crowd just stood there and cheered, and cheered, yelling itself hoarse, sharing with the madmen in Braves' uniforms the unparalleled joy of the moment. Even in the press box the normally placid newspapermen stood up and grinningly shook each other's hands. Milwaukee had never seen such a night.

12...

The citizens of Milwaukee had a whole week in which to work themselves up to a fever pitch for the World Series. The normal routine of the entire city seemed to stop in favor of the coming battle with the American League flag winners, the New York Yankees. Buses were chartered, special cars ordered to be hooked onto trains, whole plane flights were reserved in advance to accommodate the many hundreds of rabid fans who planned to follow the Braves in their invasion of Yankee Stadium. For the games to be played at County Stadium, factories and offices worked out split shifts or prepared to close entirely so that employees could attend. One city councilman proposed that the entire World Series week be declared a holiday and the schools be closed.

The Yankees, perennial American League champions, clinched their pennant the same day the Braves did theirs, so pitchers for both teams were well rested. This wasn't one of manager Casey Stengel's best Yankee teams, but it was good enough to win the pennant, and good enough to be favored by the experts to win

134

the World Series. They lined up with Bill Skowron, Joe Collins and Elston Howard sharing first base duties, Gerry Coleman at second, Gil McDougald at shortstop, Andy Carey at third with Tony Kubek as an alternate when not playing left field. With Kubek in the outfield were Hank Bauer in right and the Bronx Bombers' leading slugger, Mickey Mantle. Enos Slaughter took over in left field when Kubek played third. Yogi Berra caught a mound staff headed by Whitey Ford, Art Ditmar, Bob Turley, Bobby Shantz, Don Larsen and Tom Sturdivant.

A line of more than five hundred fans waited outside the Yankee Stadium bleacher gate the night before the Series opener. A total of 69,476 crowded in to see the opening duel between two great left-handers, Whitey Ford and Warren Spahn. For four innings Ford and Spahn matched zeroes, Spahn pitching out of trouble twice and Ford narrowly escaping in the fourth when Mathews walked and Hank singled. Each time the rallies were snuffed out without scoring.

Coleman opened the Yankees' fifth with a single. Spahn threw out Kubek, Coleman making second. Ford lined out, but Bauer doubled for the first score of the Series. After Ford again pitched out of trouble in the sixth, the Yankees chased Spahn in their half with a walk and two singles. Before Ernie Johnson could get the Yankees out two runs were across for a 3-0 Yankee lead. Ford lost his shutout in the seventh when Covington doubled and Schoendienst singled, but the Yankees were out in front with a 3-1 victory.

With the Braves' best pitcher a Yankee victim, some of the baseball experts were predicting a Yankee sweep in four games. They were forgetting that this Milwaukee team had bounced back any number of times during the season. The Braves weren't awed by the Yankees' reputation. With Burdette facing Shantz, they scored first this time, powered by Hank, who rapped a Shantz fast ball for a tremendous triple opening the second inning. Adcock backed it up with a single and the Braves had a lead.

The Yankees were no slouches at fighting back either. They came right back to tie the game in their half of the second, and only a great catch by Covington of a long drive to left field saved Burdette from further damage. Logan put the Braves ahead briefly in the third with a home run, but again the Yankees came right back to tie. An ordinary team might have been discouraged, but not this year's version of the Braves. They knocked Shantz out of the box in the next inning with a two-run rally that turned out to be the winning margin when Burdette shut out the Yankees the rest of the way.

With the Series tied, the scene shifted to Milwaukee the next day. County Stadium was draped in colorful bunting and the fans were in holiday spirit for the first World Series game ever held there. But before the first inning was over it appeared that mourning dress would have been more in order. The Yankees sent Bob Buhl to the showers before he could get the side out in the first, scoring three times, then went on

136

to a 12-3 rout, one of the worst in World Series history. Hank supplied two of the three Brave runs on a homer in the fifth inning with Logan on first.

Haney called a brief meeting in the clubhouse before the fourth game. He uttered just two lines. "After that beating yesterday their guys are expecting you to roll over and play dead. I don't think you're going to do that." He turned then and walked away.

His short but pungent talk seemed in vain an hour later when the Yankees pounced on Spahn for a run in the first inning. The left-hander settled down for the next three innings, but meanwhile Sturdivant was mowing down the Braves without trouble, making that one run look big. The huge crowd in County Stadium grew restive, sensing impending disaster unless the Braves got going.

Logan opened the bottom half of the fourth with a walk. Mathews then doubled, Logan stopping at third, and the fans began to perk up. Up to the plate stepped Hank. "Sink one!" a box seat fan yelled to him. Unblinking, Hank took Sturdivant's first pitch for a strike, then another one for a ball. The Yankee hurler worked carefully, but Hank blasted his next pitch over the left field screen for a three-run homer and a 3-1 Braves lead. Torre followed with another homer, making the score 4-1.

Working smoothly now Spahn breezed through the Yankee hitters. He had a six-hitter going into the ninth. Determined to wrap up the victory, he got Bauer on a fly ball to Hank in center field. When Mantle grounded out to Logan the fans began filing toward the exits. Berra singled next, but the fans didn't pause. They stopped short seconds later, however, when McDougald followed with another single that barely evaded Schoendienst's glove. That brought up Howard, the tying run, and sent manager Haney out to the mound. The fans booed him, wanting the popular Spahn to remain in the game, confident in the left-hander's skill. At the mound Haney talked to him briefly, patted him on the back and returned to the dugout. The crowd roared its approval.

Spahn went to a three-and-two count on Howard, then fed him a pitch that was a bit too good—Howard hit it out of the park. The score was tied, 4-4!

Stunned fans stood disbelieving in the aisles. One moment the victory had been all but assured, the next the game was tied. Spahn retired Andy Carey to end the inning. Tommy Byrne, Yankee relief pitcher, got the Braves out in order in their half of the ninth, and the game went into extra innings.

Few people in the ball park expected Spahn to pitch the tenth, for obviously he had tired suddenly, but Haney gambled with him. It seemed to Hank, standing in center field, that his usually hard-as-nails skipper might have been affected by a bit of sentimentality; Haney knew how much it meant to Spahn to redeem himself and win the game. There were a couple of relief pitchers ready and waiting, but Haney's gamble seemed like a good one when Spahn disposed of Coleman on a grounder and struck out Byrne. In a flash the picture changed again. Kubek beat out a slow roller and Bauer tripled to score him. The Yankees led now, 5-4, and Hank wondered ruefully how the second-guessers would be hanging Haney in the morning newspapers for staying with Spahn. Still the Milwaukee manager let him remain to get Mantle for the third out.

Once more the Braves had their backs to the wall, in a spot where their 1956 attitude would have persuaded them to quit. But this time they were a fighting team. Nippy Jones, pinch-hitting for Spahn, opened the Braves' tenth by being hit on the foot. Felix Mantilla went in to run for him. Bob Grim replaced Byrne on the mound for the Yankees. Schoendienst sacrificed. Logan doubled, and the tying run was in.

The crowd was screaming madly when Ed Mathews walked up to hit. The drama of the past two innings was epic. Mathews fouled the first pitch down the left field line. Then he fouled one down the right field line. Grim missed with two pitches, trying to get Mathews to swing at a bad one. Unsuccessful, he threw the next pitch over the plate, and Mathews belted it over the fence. Magically, the Braves had come back for a 7-5 victory, tying the Series again.

After that heroic finish the rest of the World Series was practically anticlimactic. Lew Burdette won his second game the next day, 1-0, on successives singles by Mathews, Hank and Adcock. They were just one game away now from the World's Championship. The Yankees, however, were veterans of too many victorious classics to give up their crown without a fight to the finish. Back in Yankee Stadium again they beat Bob Buhl, 3-2, sending the Series to its final game. Hank accounted for one of the Milwaukee runs with his third homer of the Series, a tremendous drive that soared into the bull pen in left center, several feet back of the 402-foot sign.

Spahn was due to pitch the deciding contest, but he was forced out with the flu, and Burdette was called on to try for his third win with only one day's rest. After a shaky opening inning he settled down, pitched his second straight shutout and, helped by two singles from Hank and a two-run double by Mathews, won 5-0. The Braves were World's Champions!

The team returned to Milwaukee that evening to be met with a celebration unequaled in sports history. Not since the end of World War II had Milwaukee seen such a spectacle. In ancient days victorious emperors were accorded such wild acclaim, but never a baseball team.

More than twenty thousand people swarmed over the airport waiting for the champions to land. In town, where city officials had prepared a parade and formal ceremonies, two hundred and fifty thousand more squeezed into a two block area. As the plane circled and let down its landing gear, television crews and newsreel cameramen went into action. Finally the big transport touched down, taxied and rolled to a stop at the edge of the crowd. A ramp was pushed forward through the mass of people to the door of the plane.

When it opened and manager Haney, Hank, Mathews, Burdette and the rest began to file out, the crowd broke into a roar of greeting and crashed through the police barriers. The television and newsreel crews were swamped by thousands of frantic fans rushing toward the plane. Forgotten were the prepared speeches and the ceremonies.

Milwaukee celebrated all through the night and till dawn of the next day. Brass bands paraded through the streets for hours on end, followed by prancing revelers tooting on horns and whirling noise-makers. Caravans of cars rolled through the crowds, honking their horns, trailing colored streamers. Hot dogs and soda pop were sold on the street corners all night long. Balloon and souvenir salesmen reaped a small fortune.

The first flickering rays of the morning sun lit up streets strewn with the refuse of celebration. It was only then, at morning's light, that the Braves finally managed to break away from their colossal victory party. They staggered back to their hotel, weary, disheveled and red-eyed, but unspeakably happy.

The World Series statistics were totaled the next day, pointing up Hank's vital contributions to the Braves' victories. He made virtually a clean sweep of all batting honors, leading the players of both teams in hits with eleven, homers with three, runs batted in with seven, and average with a lofty .393.

The World Series fittingly concluded Hank's finest year since entering organized baseball. During the regular season he had finished third in the league in

141

batting average, with .322, but had led the league in homers with forty-four, and in the important runs batted in department, with 132.

Soon after the Series the Baseball Writers Association of America awarded him baseball's highest seasonal award; Hank was named the Most Valuable Player in the National League for 1957.

There was one last testimonial awaiting Hank. Down in Mobile the city's leaders proclaimed a "Hank Aaron Day." Late in October, with his wife and son, he made the journey back to the city of his birth. Two thousand people were on hand to greet him when he stepped off the train. A big red and white sign said, "Welcome Home Hank." A band from one of the local high schools played "Take Me Out to the Ball Game." As photographers snapped pictures Mayor Joseph Langan of Mobile stepped forward to shake the astonished Hank's trembling hand. Then the Mayor presented him with a big gold key-to-the-city.

He had expected some kind of celebration, of course, but nothing like this. Bewildered, but deeply gratified, he allowed himself to be led by the Mayor to the front car of a hundred-car motorcade that toured Mobile's streets, lined with cheering citizens. The next day an official testimonial dinner and dance was held in his honor. He sat dazedly through the laudatory speeches at dinner, unable to comprehend that all this was for a boy from Toulminville who had hauled ice and mowed lawns for quarters not too many years ago.

He heard, dimly, the Mayor call his name, and he

stood up to accept a parchment that declared this day "Hank Aaron Day." He knew that he was expected to make some sort of speech. His throat went dry. His tongue felt too big for his mouth. What could he say? What could he say to anybody, much less all these formal-looking dignitaries and leading citizens of Mobile. The applause died down. He was there, standing. Alone. He had to say something.

"I've been a very lucky boy," he said quietly. "In the past few weeks I have received a number of honors. I have been at a lot of receptions and celebrations. But I want you all to know that for me this one is the best. This is the best . . . because this is home."

13 ...

The National League presented a strange picture when the 1958 season got under way. The Dodgers had abandoned their legendary home in Ebbets Field, Brooklyn in favor of Los Angeles, where it was presumed they would enjoy greater profits. Their traditional and storied transpontine rivals, the Giants, moved from a likewise legendary home, the Polo Grounds of Coogan's Bluff, the Bronx, thereby at once dissolving one of the most colorful intra-city rivalries in baseball history and creating a new inter-city one. Moreover, examining the trends in the league, it could readily be seen that the Dodgers had also relinquished their position as the perennial power, the "team to beat." The Milwaukee Braves, with their young World's Championship team, was talked about throughout baseball as the beginning of a new dynasty, the kind the Yankees had established so securely in the American League. They had certainly earned the prediction the way they had won the pennant and beaten the Yankees in the Series. Even owner Lou Perini was

144

prompted to remark, in the spring of 1958, "We'll be winning pennants for the next five years, at least."

The experts agreed with him. The changing geography of the league was expected to have little effect on the final standings. The Braves were outstanding favorites to repeat as pennant winners, with the Dodgers and Cardinals again the principal challengers. The Giants, new San Francisco address notwithstanding, were relegated to their usual second division berth.

By May, however, the league standings were so bizarre they defied all logic except that of the second-guessers. Sitting majestically in first place were the ill-regarded San Francisco Giants, leading the Braves. In the cellar, playing ball as though they were determined to remain there forever, were the Los Angeles Dodgers.

Nobody could figure out the Dodgers' collapse, but the Braves had an excuse. From the beginning of spring training a series of injuries attacked them like a plague. Bill Bruton didn't get to play an inning until the season was six weeks old. Schoendienst lost several weeks with a broken finger and showed signs of suffering from the tuberculosis he had contracted and that would idle him completely the following season. Wes Covington suffered knee and thigh injuries and eventually was lost for half the year. Bob Buhl missed three months and wasn't right when he finally returned. Hardly a regular didn't miss some part of the early schedule, and many were lost for a substantial part of the entire season.

Compounding the Braves' physical disabilities was

the fact that their healthiest man, Hank, was sick in his bat. In the worst slump of his career by far, he was hitting .200 at the end of May. Worse, nobody could find a flaw to blame it on.

There were any number of given possibilities for the miserable state of Hank's hitting. For a time hope spread around the National League that the pitchers had discovered some major weak spot in his batting style. It was much more likely, however, that a combination of three unrelated factors was responsible for his slump. First and probably least important, he was bothered with an infected tooth and didn't want to take the time to have it treated. The other two factors were greater problems, each perhaps equally burdening him.

In December, months before the season opened, his wife gave birth in Milwaukee to twin sons, whom they named Gary and Larry. Two days later Gary died. Hank and his wife understandably were deeply grieved by the loss. It took a great deal of time before they were able to shake off the effect of the shock. This was one of the things that weighed on Hank's mind in the spring days of the 1958 season; it affected his ability to concentrate on the pitch, took the minutest fraction of a second off his timing—enough to ruin his hitting.

Were that not enough, it was the opinion of many close followers of the Braves, including the sports writers, that Hank was trying to live up to his 1957-earned reputation as a home run hitter. "He's guessing wrong, taking too many called strikes waiting for a fat pitch to belt," they said. And, "He's not swinging freely the way he used to. He's pressing too hard trying to blast everything out of the park."

There was some statistical evidence to support this. As poorly as Hank was hitting, he still managed to break open an occasional ball game with a homer. In a period of eight games, while failing to raise his average one point, he hit five homers to win three of the four games the Braves chalked up that week. First he conquered the Pirates with a three-run homer in a 5-3 game. Then two homers and a single beat the Phillies, 6-3. The next day, opening a series against the Giants, he homered in the first inning for a 2-0 lead, then, in the ninth, with the Braves losing 6-4, he hit a three-run homer to save the game. In between homers he went practically hitless.

Fortunately for the Braves the amazing Giants did not have the pitching or the power to open a substantial lead, and as it did in 1957, the Milwaukee bench came through in high style. Juggling his men in the best tradition of Casey Stengel, who was perhaps the master juggler of all baseball managers, Haney kept his team in contention when everything was breaking badly. The Braves never fell more than three games behind. Using liberally such reserves as Felix Mantilla, Andy Pafko, young Mel Roach, Harry Hanebrink and Frank Torre, he kept the Braves together. With Buhl's arm gone sore and Lew Burdette suddenly ineffective, Haney plugged the holes in his mound staff

147

with youngsters Joey Jay, Carlton Willey and Juan Pizzaro. At one point, when second baseman Schoendienst and his replacement Roach both were injured, Haney sent Hank back to his old position for a couple of days, winding up with three outfielders playing the infield—Mantilla, Hanebrink and Adcock.

Never particularly auspicious as an infielder, Hank nevertheless performed creditably at second for three days. When he was restored to the outfield the sports writers asked him how he had felt being back at second, first praising him for his adaptability. "You looked good out there," one said to him. "A Frankie Frisch you're not, but you played a good second base."

Hank shrugged. "A couple of days don't mean anything. You see me play second a few games, you think I'm a major leaguer out there. But I'm not. I'm not kidding anybody. I'm an outfielder and it was lucky for me the Braves switched me right away. Besides, they ought to pay infielders more money. It's a lot harder than being an outfielder. I didn't like it one bit."

Going into the last week in June Hank was still hitting a meager .254. Getting desperate, Haney asked special batting coach Paul Waner to take a long, close look at Hank's hitting style with a view toward perhaps making some changes. "Maybe the pitchers have found some flaw we don't know about," he said to Waner. "See what you can see."

No better man than Waner could he have found for such a job. In the 1930's, playing for the Pittsburgh Pirates, Paul and his brother Lloyd were the terrors

148

of National League hitting. Paul Waner was known as "Big Poison," Lloyd was "Little Poison." Paul was an expert at place hitting, specializing in Wee Willie Keeler's famous philosophy, "Hit 'em where they ain't." He had a trick, in batting practice, of placing a number of baseball caps around the outfield then demonstrating how close to them he could make a batted ball drop. Often as not he would place a hit squarely on top of his target.

So if any man would spot a flaw in a batting style it would be Paul Waner. He watched Hank closely in batting practice and in the next three ball games. He returned to Haney then with his report. "Anybody who tampers with Aaron's swing ought to have his head examined," Waner said. "Leave him alone. He'll break out of his slump. He'll find the groove again all by himself, like every great hitter does eventually."

On June 25, in a game against the Giants, Hank broke out. It didn't look like much to begin with. He singled in his last two turns at bat. That began a spree of eleven base hits in his next thirteen at bats and a long upward surge that didn't stop until he was batting in his normal atmosphere, well over .300. As Waner had predicted he had straightened himself out. As the reason for his slump was difficult to define, so was the reason for his awakening. The bad tooth was still abscessed and uncared for, further evidence that this was a minor annoyance; apparently Hank had managed to dislodge the depression that had weighed over him heavily since the death of his two-day-old son, and

149

had come to the realization that trying to hit home runs was the surest way to an anemic batting average.

In the one month of July he boosted his average nearly eighty points with a hitting rampage that had National League pitchers chewing their nails in frustration. A pitcher who held him to two hits a game considered himself fortunate. Doubles and triples boomed off the fences, and, without deliberately trying to, he found himself hitting as many homers as he had before. Against the Dodgers one day in July he hit a grand-slam homer and three singles, and the fact that the Braves won the game 7-6 indicated how important was Hank's role in the victory. There was just no getting him out.

One of the better pitchers in the league described that summer how he felt about pitching to Hank. After several great years with the Dodgers Don Newcombe, traded in June of 1958 to the Redlegs, was asked by his fellow moundsmen if he had any special way of pitching to Hank. Newcombe just groaned. "Aaron? I wish I could pitch him *under* the plate!"

Curiously, baseball history repeated itself as the pennant race moved into the month of August. In 1957, at this point, the Braves broke the race open with a big winning streak at the same time their closest rivals fell into slumps. Now again, at almost precisely the same date, the race was a tight one. But not for long. On July 30 the Braves were in second place, a game behind the Giants. Only seven games behind were the seventh place Phillies. The Dodgers remained bogged in the cellar.

Then the Braves began to move. They beat the Dodgers two straight while the Giants lost two to the Redlegs. Now Milwaukee had the league lead by one game and a four-game series with the Giants coming up. The next three days in San Francisco's Candlestick Park could be crucial ones.

"If we can take three out of the four," Haney told them on the plane northward, "we're sitting pretty. Take all four games and we can forget about the Giants and maybe the rest of the league too."

Haney had Burdette and Willey scheduled for the first two games, with Spahn and young Pizzaro slated for the Sunday double-header. Manager Bill Rigney of the Giants was ready to counter with Johnny Antonelli, Ramon Monzant, Ruben Gomez and Mike McCormick. What packed the ball park for the four-game series— which had the elements of a World Series in excitement—was not the prospective pitching duals, however. The fans hoped to see an explosive hitting contest between two of the game's great outfielders—Hank and the Giants' Willie Mays.

But it was Burdette and Antonelli who controlled the first six innings of the opening game. Each was pitching a sparkling three-hit shutout as the Braves came to bat in the seventh. Leading off, Schoendienst singled. Mathews followed with another single. Hank then hit Antonelli's first pitch for a double to right center field, scoring both runners. Antonelli was re-

151

placed by Stu Miller, who got Covington on a pop fly, but Adcock singled Hank home before Miller got the side out.

Burdette rolled along on his 3-0 lead through the seventh and into two outs in the eighth before Mays delighted the Candlestick Park patrons with a two-run homer. Hank countered with a homer in the ninth to make the score 4-2, and Burdette wrapped it up, striking out the Giants in order in the bottom of the ninth.

Carlton Willey and Hank continued the conquest of the Giants in the second game. Effectively stopping Mays, the Milwaukee hurler pitched a masterful shutout while Hank kept the pressure off him with a first inning home run followed by a double and two singles. It was a 10-0 rout.

The double-header had the ball park crowded to the rafters. The Giant fans as well as the Giants themselves knew that these were vital contests. They had to win at least one of the games to remain in pennant contention.

Mays helped pitcher Gomez to an early lead, hitting Spahn for a three-run homer in the first inning. The star left-hander of the Braves steadied after that, but Gomez was pitching superbly. Hank singled in the second to no avail and Bruton doubled in the fourth for the only two hits off Gomez in the first six innings. In the seventh inning Mathews homered, making the score 3-1. Mays got that one back when he doubled, stole third and scored on a fly ball. So it was 4-1 in the ninth inning when the roof fell in on Gomez. Pinch-hitting for Spahn, Pafko singled. Bruton singled and Schoendienst walked, loading the bases. Rigney came off the bench to talk to Gomez, but let him remain, and the pitcher obliged by striking out Mathews. That brought up Hank. The Giant fans in the stands screamed at Gomez to get him out. The Braves' slugger stood at the plate, quietly menacing. Gomez wound up and threw a curve for a strike. Two more curves were outside, then Gomez switched to a fast ball over the inside corner. Hank swung—and the Giant fans groaned. Outfielder Jackie Brandt ran back a couple of steps then watched helplessly as the ball sailed out of the park for a grand-slam home run. With one swing of his bat Hank had switched the score to 5-4 in the Braves' favor. Aroused now, they sent three more runs across the plate before the inning was over, winning the game 8-4.

The Giants were down now to their last game. A loss would not only put them five games behind, but into a tie for third place with the fast-climbing Pittsburgh Pirates. Two young pitchers were on the mound, Pizzaro for the Braves and McCormick for the Giants, and though each pitched creditably it was the sluggers, Mays and Hank, who dominated the play and drew the cheers of the crowd.

Hank began the heroics with a homer, leading off the second inning. Accepting the challenge as clean-up hitter for the Giants, Mays did the same in the Giants' half of the second. Pizzaro got into further trouble when Felipe Alou and Bill White followed with sin-

153

gles. Recalled from the Wichita farm team just two weeks earlier Pizzaro was shaken up. He threw a fast ball too good to Darryl Spencer, who rifled it deep to left center field. The crowd roared. It looked like a certain double, perhaps a triple. Running frantically to his right, his back half turned to the plate, Hank pursued the ball. His spikes churned up the turf as he ran, but it appeared the ball would drop in safely. At the last moment he leaped forward and stuck out his glove. Incredibly he made a backhand stab of the ball, but tipping forward off balance he went tumbling head over heels on the outfield grass. In a flash he was up on his feet, however, triumphantly holding up the ball he had managed to retain for the out. Alou and White scrambled back to their bases.

On the mound Pizzaro drew a deep breath. Had that ball gone through it would have knocked him out of the ball game and quite possibly right back to the minor leagues. But heartened now by Hank's miraculous save, and given the moment to settle down, he got out of the inning without further scoring.

The tie held until the fifth inning. Then Mathews singled and Hank doubled for a run. Torre walked and Hanebrink sent a tremendous drive to center field. Not to be outdone by his Milwaukee counterpart Mays ran back and made a sensational over-the-shoulder catch on the run. Mantilla hit into a double play to end the threat, but the Braves led, 2-1.

It was Hank and Mays again in the seventh sending the crowd into shouts of delight. Hank opened the inning with his third straight hit, a single. Torre doubled to left, and when Brandt fumbled momentarily, Hank swung around third and headed for home. Recovering quickly Brandt threw a perfect strike to catcher White, who waited crouching, blocking the plate. Hank slid home hard, a fraction of a second after the ball plunked into White's mitt. The catcher and the runner tumbled together in a cloud of dust. The umpire peered into the tangle, jerked his thumb up in the "out" sign, but then switched to "safe" as he saw the ball trickle away, bounced out of White's grasp by Hank's bruising slide.

Torre meanwhile continued on to third and scored on a fly ball by Hanebrink. The score was now 4-1. McCormick got the next two Braves and the Giants' turn came to bat. Jim Davenport led off with a bunt single. Orlando Cepeda, who was to win the Rookie of the Year award, followed with a double, Davenport holding at third. That brought up Mays, the tying run. The Giant center fielder, one of the all-time greats, had not yet won the popularity of the new fans in San Francisco, but now they cheered and stamped their feet as he crashed a home run that knotted the score again.

Into the ninth inning the score remained 4-4. The Giants were reeling along the ropes. The Braves were applying the pressure, anxious for a knock-out. Bruton began the ninth beating out an infield single. Schoendienst sacrificed. Mathews then golfed a sizzling line drive down the third base line that looked like a hit, but Davenport leaped at the ball and knocked it down. Halfway down to third on the hit, Bruton was caught in a rundown and tagged out, but with his speed he managed to delay the tag until Mathews ran around to second. With two out now Hank stepped up to hit.

Manager Rigney called time and ran out to the mound, signaling to catcher White to join him for a conference. "Keep the ball low and outside," he said to his battery. "Throw all curves. Walk him if you have to, first base is open anyway. But don't give this guy anything good to hit!"

McCormick and White nodded their assent and Rigney ran back to the dugout. The Giant pitcher went to work on Hank with low outside curves, missing the first two for called balls. Hank looked down at the third base coach for a sign and got the okay to hit away if the pitch was good. He sensed that McCormick was under orders to keep the ball away from his power, to walk him rather than throw him a good pitch. They were hoping he would bite at a bad one and make an out.

As McCormick came down with the third outside curve Hank leaned forward a fraction and inched his toes closer to the plate. The curve from the left-hand pitcher broke low and outside, but nevertheless in toward right-handed hitting Hank. He swung, ready for the pitch, and sliced it down the right field foul line for a double, Mathews scoring the tie-breaker. Covington fouled out, but the Braves had the Giants down, with half an inning to go.

The Giants, or at least certainly Willie Mays, were not quite ready to be counted out. Pizzaro disposed of the first two batters. Then Mays came up. In center field Hank moved back several steps, reflecting ruefully that it seemed Mays came up every time a vital moment was at hand. Then he smiled to himself, with some deserved pride, recalling that a sports writer had quoted manager Bill Rigney saying that same thing about him a few days ago.

Typically, Mays came through with a single. On the first pitch to Alou he broke for second. Knowing of his tremendous speed and daring on the bases the Braves were anticipating him, but Alou swung and looped a hit to right field. Bruton sped over, cut the ball off and threw accurately to the plate, but Mays, one of the few men in baseball able to score from first on a single, did the trick again to tie the score.

Alou went to second on Bruton's throw to the plate but Pizzaro pitched out of further trouble, sending the game into extra innings.

By the twelfth inning Joey Jay had replaced Pizzaro and Rigney had brought in Antonelli, his leading starter, to relieve McCormick. Antonelli never got a man out. Schoendienst singled, Mathews walked and Hank tripled off the wall. Gomez warmed up hurriedly and took over, getting Covington on a long fly ball that scored Hank, and the next two men on strike-outs. Three runs were in, and Jay came on in the last of the twelfth to retire the Giants in order, and the San Franciscans were all but eliminated from the pennant race.

157

The Braves were five games in front of the Giants and Pirates, but not yet home free. A suddenly and strangely aroused, lightly regarded Pittsburgh team rose up to threaten them. In Milwaukee at the end of August the Pirates opened a four-game series with a 4-3 win, climbing to within four games of the top. A sweep of the next three and they'd be just one game behind with momentum on their side. But they didn't even win one. Burdette beat them, 6-1, then Willey, 2-1, and finally Spahn, 3-2, on a bases-loaded double by Hank. The Braves had beaten back another challenge. It was the last one of the season.

There remained now, in the waning days of September, just the pennant clincher. Again it took place before an hysterical crowd in County Stadium. Again, as in 1957, the game was a spine-tingler climaxed by the unbelievable heroics of Hank Aaron.

For six innings, seeking his twenty-first victory, Warren Spahn had set down the Redlegs with one hit. Meanwhile, Hank had doubled home two runs in the fourth inning and Mathews had homered for two more in the sixth for a 4-0 lead. Then Frank Robinson led off the Redlegs' seventh with a home run, and before Don McMahon could come in and stop the rally, four more runs crossed the plate for a 5-4 Redlegs lead.

In the Braves half of the seventh Mathews singled, and an expectant roar rose from the crowd as Hank walked up to the plate. They stamped their feet, whistled and cheered, then broke into a frenzy of shouts and applause as Hank came through once more, hitting a tremendous home run that provided the tying and lead runs. McMahon blanked the Redlegs the rest of the way, and the Braves had their second straight pennant.

The clubhouse later was full of grins and back-slapping, of course, but the atmosphere was far more subdued than the wild victory celebration of the year before. Hank and Spahn and McMahon came in for most of the photo-taking and handshaking. As he posed in front of his locker with his teammates, Hank tried to express to the sports writers how he and the Braves felt. "We're World's Champions now," he said. "We know how to win like champions."

14...

The Braves were brash champions going into the 1958 World Series against the Yankees. They had a right to be. For the second straight season they had won the pennant handily, by eight games, despite a multitude of injuries. On the other hand, the Yankees, though winning their pennant by ten games, were a far cry from the Yankees of old. They captured the pennant with only ninety-two victories—the same total as the Braves—but this was the lowest victory total in the Stengel era of Yankee teams. Luckily the American League was a weak one, and they won easily despite the fact that they lost more games than they won through August and September.

Even Stengel was prompted to say about them, "They're not one of the best teams I've had here. They drop fly balls in the outfield, they don't hit with men on base and the infield has become erratic."

The team line-ups were virtually the same as those fielded in the 1957 Series, making the Braves slight favorites for this one. The Milwaukee fans gave their team a tremendous street parade on the eve of the

160

opening game, cheering the Braves and imploring them to "do it again."

Both the experts and the fans were ignoring the fact that no National League team had won two consecutive World Series since the Giants of 1921-1922.

Ignoring the percentages himself, manager Haney bypassed Burdette, who had beaten the Yankees three times in the 1957 classic, and started his big winner of the season, Spahn. He also sidelined Bill Bruton, put veteran Andy Pafko in center field and moved Hank into right. Stengel named Whitey Ford as his first game starter.

For three innings the two left-handers matched scoreless frames. Then, with two out in the fourth Moose Skowron homered for a 1-0 Yankee lead. The Braves came right back in their half of the fourth. Hank waited out one of his infrequent walks and moved to second on a passed ball. Adcock then grounded out, sending him on to third, where he scored the tying run on a single by Crandall. Pafko singled, Logan popped out for the second out, but Spahn helped himself to a lead with a single, scoring Crandall.

Bauer homered with one on in the fifth to give the Yankees a one-run edge again. In the eighth Mathews walked and Hank followed with a double, tying the score. It remained a 3-3 game until the tenth when singles by Adcock, Crandall and Bruton, pinch-hitting for Pafko, won the game 4-3.

Five Yankee pitchers took a savage beating in the

161

second game. Just half an hour after the game began it appeared as though the Braves had indeed superseded the Yankees as the power in baseball. Schoendienst opened the contest with a single, Bruton walked, Mathews singled, Hank doubled, and pitcher Bob Turley was headed for an early shower. Duke Maas and Johnny Kucks didn't fare much better in that inning, seven runs scoring. It was more than enough for Burdette, who was able to coast along, homers by Bauer and Mickey Mantle hardly bothering him. His teammates continued their slugging against relief pitchers Murry Dickson and Zach Monroe, Hank starting a rally in the seventh with his second double. Final score was Braves 13, Yankees 5.

The Series moved to the Yankee Stadium, where a large contingent of fans from Milwaukee settled down, dreaming of a four-game sweep by the Braves. Bob Rush, the veteran ex-Cub, was Haney's choice, and while he pitched well enough to win most games, the Braves didn't hit for him. Don Larsen, who in 1956 had pitched the only perfect no-hitter in Series history, set the Braves down with just six singles up to the seventh inning, when he appeared to be tiring, and Ryne Duren came in to complete his shutout.

One of the masterpieces of World Series pitching was unfolded in the fifth game. Striking out seven, allowing just four balls to be hit to the outfield, Spahn pitched a 3-0, two-hit shutout. Only four better performances had ever been recorded in a World Series—Larsen's 1956 no-hitter, and three previous one-hitters.

Spahn's two-hitter was only the fourteenth in World Series history.

In Milwaukee the fans and the city fathers began warming up a victory celebration. The Braves themselves were confident, but cautious. Only one club had ever come back from a 3-1 deficit to win a World Series —the 1925 Pittsburgh Pirates. Poised on the brink of an unprecedented second straight Series defeat, the Yankees came back behind Bob Turley in the fifth game, winning 7-0. Still, they needed two more consecutive victories to regain the championship.

Three singles by Hank and a fine pitching job by Spahn couldn't nail down the Series in the sixth game. After Bauer homered in the first inning, the Braves gave their thirty-seven-year-old left-hander a 2-1 edge, aided by a bit of shrewd batting tactics on the part of Hank.

With Ed Mathews on third in the fourth inning, and Ford's control effectively keeping the ball away from his power, Hank suddenly pulled a bunt toward third, where he caught Andy Carey playing deep. Carey recovered quickly, scooped up the ball and threw to first —there was no play possible on Mathews. The ball and Hank arrived together, but the throw was on the home plate side of the base line. Skowron had to lean in and across the base path to catch the ball, and Hank, charging down the line, crashed full speed into the burly first baseman, sending him flying, without the ball. The tying run was across, Hank was on first, and Ford was so shaken by Hank's nervy play, he let Cov-

163

ington reach him for a double. Hank came all the way around with the lead run.

The 2-1 lead looked as though it would hold up the way Spahn was going. But a break made the difference for the Yankees. In the sixth inning Mantle singled. Howard followed with a single, and when Bruton fumbled Mantle went around to third. Berra followed with a sacrifice fly, Mantle scoring the tying run after the catch. Had Bruton not fumbled, Mantle would have been forced to hold at second base, would not have been in position to score on Berra's fly ball, and the Braves would have won.

As it was, Spahn and relief pitcher Duren kept pace through the regulation nine innings. The game went to the tenth, 2-2. Spahn walked out to the mound to pitch the top of the tenth, his twenty-ninth inning in this Series, a new record. But the record had its price. Gil McDougald opened the tenth with a home run, Bauer and Mantle were retired, but Berra and Howard singled. Haney replaced Spahn with McMahon, and as the game left-hander slowly walked from the mound a thunderous ovation from the Milwaukee fans followed him.

Skowron greeted McMahon with another single, making the score 4-2. The Braves fought back with one run in their half of the tenth, not enough to prevent the Yankees from tying the Series at three games each.

The pressure shifted to the Braves now. Though each team tottered equally on the brink, the Yankees were accustomed to it. This was the fourth straight year they had been involved in a seven-game Series. Heart-thumping tension gripped crowded County Stadium in that seventh game, the excitement and suspense growing with every pitch as the game went through seven innings a 2-2 tie.

In the eighth inning, with two out, Berra doubled and Howard singled him home with the tie-breaking run. Carey singled, and when Skowron hit one over the left field fence the hush in County Stadium was more eloquent than words. There was barely a person there who didn't realize it was all over but the necessary nine innings. Minutes later Bob Turley got the final out. The Yankees had reclaimed in true professional style their World's Championship.

It was little consolation to Hank that he was singled out by the sports writers for his outstanding play in the Series. He had hit .333, his nine hits tying him for high on the club with Schoendienst. Added to his regular season average of .326, with thirty homers and ninety-five runs batted in, it made for another superb season.

15...

In the Los Angeles Dodgers' dugout, on a day late in May of the 1959 baseball season, the conversation came around to Hank Aaron. "I see that Aaron went three-for-three against the Cards last night," pitcher Don Drysdale said to first baseman Gil Hodges.

"What's he hitting now?" Hodges asked.

Drysdale looked down at the morning newspaper he had been reading. "Four sixty-two."

"Four sixty-two," Hodges repeated, shaking his head. "The guy's impossible."

"How come he only got up three times though?" Duke Snider asked. "He walk?"

Drysdale nodded. "Y'know, if that Aaron would wait out walks like Ted Williams he'd hit four hundred I bet."

"True," said Hodges, "but I think it's the fact that he won't wait that maybe makes him a tougher hitter than Williams. Or even Musial. At least a pitcher knows with those two that if he works carefully, figuring on walking them if he has to, he can get away with it. Aaron'll hit anything he can reach. Right, Don?"

Drysdale smiled ruefully. "Right. I remember a game couple of weeks ago when he ruined me that way. We were winning by one run, and they had a guy on second—Mathews I think—and it was two out. I worked the corners on Aaron, figuring I'd rather walk him with first base open than give him something good to hit. In a spot like that Musial would have walked on what I threw. I never pitched against Williams but they tell me his eyes are so good and he's such a batting machine he don't swing if the ball's half an inch off the plate. But not Aaron. I swear he swung at a pitch that was six inches off the plate. And what'd he do with it? Hit it to right center for a double. A guy like that wears out a pitcher."

"With all due respect for the guys on our club," said the veteran Hodges, "I think Aaron will be the best hitter in baseball for the next ten years."

The Dodgers were hardly the only ones discussing Hank that spring. From opening day when his three hits beat the Phillies, he was on a hitting rampage bordering on the impossible. For three weeks he was hitting .500, then, at a stage when one bad day at the plate could drop an average twenty points, he continued on for another month batting above .450. As the Dodgers had discussed, he had only thirteen walks in his first forty games, an incredibly low total for a .450 hitter.

Comparisons with Musial, Williams, Mantle and Mays were frequent. With Musial and Williams then in the twilight of their great careers, it was obvious that Hank was one of the three hitters who figured to dominate the major leagues for the next decade. How he rated with the Giant and Yankee stars was a matter of often violent opinion. Purists claimed his insistence on swinging at bad pitches was a serious fault. Others claimed this was one of his prime assets.

In any case his .462 average late in May made him the target of an avalanche of publicity. He was hounded by newsmen, television interviewers, photographers, and pitchmen seeking his endorsement of products. Hank didn't want any of it, but he recalled all too well that in the past his reluctance to talk had resulted in droll stories that plagued him to this day. Accordingly, when he was cornered by sports writer Roger Kahn in the lobby of Philadelphia's Hotel Warwick one day, he agreed to an interview over breakfast.

"What kind of story you gonna write?" he said to Kahn.

"It's hard to say until I write it," Kahn responded.

"Listen," Hank said, "if you hear a lot of silly things about me, ask me about 'em before you write. I know what happened and what didn't."

"Your batting average will be part of what I write, and that's not silly," Kahn said.

Hank shook his head. "I mean a guy once wrote something about me—it wasn't much, but there was a lot of dumb stuff. Like everytime I said 'I' he spelled it 'Ah.'"

Kahn nodded his head in understanding. "I mean,"

Hank continued, "this isn't gonna be one of those Uncle Tom stories, is it?"

"No," Kahn said sincerely.

"In that case I'll cooperate with you," Hank said. "I don't like those Uncle Tom stories. They're all wrong and they never happened—that stuff about not knowing Ford Frick and Robin Roberts and all that dumb junk."

Hank was breathing hard now, having relieved himself once and for all—and for the first time publicly—of a burden he had carried since his rookie year in organized baseball. He was not only a mature hitter now, he was a mature person.

The momentum provided by Hank's amazing hitting carried the Braves along in first place through the months of spring. But in the front office of the ball club, and among a number of the more knowledgeable baseball writers, there was an unaccountable feeling of something wrong somewhere. It was Birdie Tebbetts, former manager of the Redlegs and new Milwaukee vice president, who first expressed his feelings out loud. A sports writer had asked him how serious he thought was the loss of Schoendienst, who was home ill with tuberculosis.

"Everybody is talking about our hole at second base," sighed Tebbetts, "but there's something else that bothers me more. We are too set a ball club. I wish there were some kids capable of giving the older men a fight for a job."

169

"Are you implying there's a feeling of complacency on this team?" said the writer.

Tebbetts winced. He remembered that the charge had been leveled against the 1956 Braves when they lost the pennant. Still, he had to say what had to be said. "That's right, I'm talking about complacency," he admitted. "But it's a different kind than the complacency they say hurt the 1956 club. Then, nobody thought they could win the pennant and they were content to ride along as a runner-up. This time they feel so darn secure about their jobs and the fact they're going to win a pennant that I feel they're not using their abilities to the utmost. A hungry team is a scrappy team. And this team isn't scrappy."

"Don't you think you'll win the pennant then?"

"Sure I think so," Tebbetts said. "But I tell you what else worries me. Only once in the last thirty years has a club won three pennants in a row in this league."

In truth there was much more to worry about than Tebbetts cared to acknowledge. The loss of Schoendienst was doubly serious. The Braves had lost more than a fine second baseman. They lost a leader. He had stepped in two seasons earlier and unified the whole team, had smoothed the infield's play to a machine-like precision. In his absence there was readily discernible a certain looseness, an unsureness of play. The Braves tried frantically to find a suitable replacement. They tried Mantilla, they brought up from the minors Casey Wise and Johnny O'Brien, they even

170

bought Bobby Avila from the Boston Red Sox. None of them were really adequate.

Pitching presented another problem. As usual Spahn and Burdette were superb, Bob Buhl was good as a third starter, but the vaunted depth of their pitching staff proved to be quite shallow. Promising youngsters such as Pizzaro, Willey and Jay failed time after time. So did Bob Rush.

Only the offense was there. Hank was magnificent. Mathews, Adcock and Logan also were outstanding contributors. It was they who made the Braves go, combining their hitting with the pitching duet of Spahn and Burdette.

At the All-Star game break in early July the Braves held a slim half game lead over the Giants and one game over the Dodgers. Still hitting at an astronomical .375, Hank was given an All-Star honor more than merely rare—it was unprecedented. He became the first player to receive a unanimous vote for any major league All-Star team. Considering the fact that the balloting was done by the National League players, coaches and managers, it was a solid tribute by the men who played against him.

In midsummer of 1959 manager Haney began to experience the same uneasy feeling that must have dogged Charley Grimm in 1956. The newspapers and magazines suddenly appeared to be filled with criticisms of his managing, carrying with the multitude of rumors and opinions the quotes of the Braves' management giving him a vote of confidence. Haney knew, as Grimm knew before him and every baseball manager knows, that he was therefore on the spot with his bosses. If the Braves failed to win the 1959 pennant out he would go. His fault or not, he realized that it was part of the manager's job to take the blow of the axe on his neck when a sacrificial goat was needed.

By September the Braves had slipped to third place, but remained close to the league-leading Giants and the second place Dodgers. Three games separated the three teams. It was going to be a neck-and-neck race all the way. The fans exulted, looking forward to an exciting month of baseball.

The Braves weren't helped any by the loss of Covington and Logan to injuries. Schoendienst tried to make a comeback in September, but it was apparent that he was not yet ready to play. They obtained veteran Enos Slaughter from the Yankees, hoping for some timely pinch-hitting, but the days moved on and they could make no progress. They won seven straight in mid month, but all three teams were playing sensational ball; the best they could do was move up into a tie for second with the Dodgers.

They were down now to the final week of the season, and suddenly the Giants fell apart, the way the Braves had in 1956. The Dodgers beat them three straight, dropping them to third place. The Braves kept pace, tying the Dodgers for the league lead.

With three games left to play the Dodgers pulled ahead, beating the Cubs while the Braves lost to the Phillies. Two games left; the tension and pressure were

172

mounting on the Braves. Warren Spahn started the next to last game of the season, pitching against Robin Roberts. As the Braves ran out of their dugout to take their positions for the game, they got a flash from Chicago that Alvin Dark of the Cubs had hit a three-run homer in the second inning. The Milwaukee players took heart.

"Let's go get 'em!" shouted Joe Adcock.

Gene Freese got the Phillies out in front, however, hitting Spahn for a home run in the second inning. The Braves got that one back in their half of the inning, but Spahn yielded another homer in the fourth, to Wally Post, for a 2-1 Phillies lead. From Chicago came word that the Cubs had scored six more times and were leading the Dodgers 9-0. It looked like a loss for certain for Los Angeles; a victory for the Braves would tie the pennant race again.

Mathews opened the Braves' fourth with a single. Hank followed with another single. Adcock sacrificed. Lee Maye, a rookie brought up to replace Covington, was walked intentionally. Avila hit into a force play at second, and Mathews came home with the tying run.

Through the fifth, sixth and seventh Roberts and Spahn battled. The Milwaukee hurler had an extra incentive going for him. He was looking for the 267th win of his career, which would be a new National League record for left handers.

In the bottom of the eighth Roberts got Spahn and Bruton, but Mathews singled. Hank then rapped Roberts' first pitch for a double into the left field corner, scoring Mathews with what proved to be the winning run. The Braves were tied for first.

On the last day of the season they beat the Phils again, but the Dodgers won the game against the Cubs. The pennant race ended in a tie.

A three-game playoff began the next day in Milwaukee. Carlton Willey opposing Danny McDevitt of the Dodgers. Willey got a bad break in the first inning when a grounder by Charley Neal took a bad hop past Avila for a hit. Neal moved to second on an infield out and scored on a single by Norm Larker.

The Braves took a 2-1 lead in the second inning, chasing McDevitt with three straight singles. Larry Sherry took over for McDevitt, and the Dodger relief star allowed but one Brave to reach first thereafter. He walked Hank. At that the 2-1 lead would have held up, but in the third another bouncer got through Avila, costing a run and tying the score. In the sixth, catcher Johnny Roseboro homered, providing the Dodgers with a 3-2 victory.

The playoffs moved to Los Angeles the next day for a thriller of shattering proportions. Manager Fred Haney poured twenty-two men into the line-up and the Dodgers' Walter Alston used twenty, each pilot platooning men in and out through the grueling twelve-inning contest.

This time the Braves jumped into the lead. After Bruton began the game by striking out, Mathews walked. Hank doubled him home for the first run, then scored the second one on a single by Torre. The Dodg-

ers got one of the runs back in their half of the first
on a triple by Neal and a single by Wally Moon. The
Braves made it 3-1 in a second when Logan and Burdette singled, Logan scoring on a throwing error by
Duke Snider.

Neal homered for the Dodgers in the fourth, but
when Mathews countered with a homer in the fifth and
the Braves scored one more in the eighth, it looked like
a certain win for Burdette. Into the bottom of the ninth
he was going strong with a 5-2 lead.

Moon started the Dodgers off in the ninth with a
single. Snider singled, Hodges singled and only a fast
cut-off and throw by Hank kept Moon on third. Burdette was finished, however. McMahon came in from
the bull pen, and was promptly greeted by a two-run
single by Larker. That made the score 5-4 and brought
Spahn in hastily to replace McMahon. Carl Furillo,
batting for Roseboro, flied to left field, scoring Hodges
with the tying run.

When Maury Wills singled, Spahn came out and
Joey Jay took over. Haney wasn't giving any pitcher
very much rope—star or not. He had a game, a pennant
and a job riding with every pitch. Jay got pinch-hitter
Ron Fairly to end the rally.

The pennant now was down as close as it could possibly get—extra innings of a playoff game. The fans
were hoarse with screaming. Every pitch, every swing
was the signal for a cheer or a groan. They played
through the tenth, through the eleventh. In the top of
the twelfth Hank walked with two out. Dodger relief

pitcher Stan Williams had pitched him so carefully he couldn't find even a bad pitch reasonably good enough to swing at. Williams, hurling hitless ball since the tenth, got Torre to snuff out the brief threat.

Pitching the twelfth for Milwaukee, Rush disposed of Moon and Williams. But Hodges walked, and catcher Joe Pignatano singled him to third. Furillo hit a sharp grounder through the middle. Desperately Mantilla scooted over for it, stopped it, but threw to first off balance. The throw went through Torre on a wild hop and Hodges streaked home with the pennant winning run.

Two days later Haney "resigned" as manager. The most elementary student of baseball knew that he hadn't jumped. He was pushed.

The post mortems were long and loud. Defenders of Haney mostly pointed to the final standings. "It took a playoff to beat him," they said. His detractors argued that there should never have been a playoff; that with proper managing the Braves would have won by as much as ten games. He was too conservative, he didn't give the young pitchers a chance, he bunted too much and didn't run enough. One of the most vociferous of the Haney critics was shortstop Johnny Logan. When Haney announced his resignation Logan let loose a long diatribe.

"Anybody but Haney could have managed us to a pennant," he exclaimed. "You can bet that very few guys on this club were sorry to see him go." He followed with a list of errors in managing he claimed against Haney. "Did we have a slow club? Were we slow runners?" the angry shortstop cried. "Mathews and Aaron can really fly. Did Haney ever run with them? He bats Mathews second and Aaron third. Who bats a home run hitter like Mathews second and a perfect clean-up hitter like Aaron third? Mathews hits forty-six homers and only bats in a hundred and fourteen runs. What kind of managing is that?"

Naturally the sports writers followed up Logan's outburst by asking the other players how they felt. The young pitchers sided with Logan, claiming that it was true that Haney showed no confidence in them, squelching their spirit. The majority of the veterans were more guarded in their statements.

"I don't know who Logan was speaking for but it wasn't me," Hank said. "Haney treated me like a man. People may blame the manager when the team doesn't win the pennant, but not the players. Sure, Haney didn't let me run as much as I wanted to sometimes, but that was part of the job."

How the Braves' management felt about Haney's alleged conservative baseball was perhaps most clearly demonstrated in their selection of Charlie Dressen as his replacement. A less conservative manager would have been difficult to find. A coach with the Dodgers in 1959, Dressen had behind him a long career in both leagues as manager, coach and umpire-baiter. Noisy and colorful, he twice won pennants with the Dodgers in the early 1950's, and twice had been thrown out of baseball temporarily. An engaging egotist, he loudly claimed a good part of credit for the Dodgers' 1959 triumph in the pennant race and World Series.

"The Dodgers will be even better in 1960," he said after taking the Milwaukee post. "But so will the Braves. I got plenty of patchwork to do, but we'll win it easy."

There was at least one spot on the Braves Dressen knew needed no patching, and that was right field. After his monumental first two months Hank naturally had dropped his batting average to human levels, but even there it was good enough to gain him his second batting championship. He hit .355 in 1959, was third in the league in homers with thirty-nine, and third in runs batted in with one hundred twenty-three.

16 . . .

Charlie Dressen did work many wonders his first season in Milwaukee. He even got a rise out of imperturbable Hank Aaron. "I understand there's a second base problem here," he said in spring training. "Well, if we can't solve it any other way, I can solve it by moving in Aaron from the outfield."

"I'll play second," said Hank, raising a laconic eyebrow when he heard about it, "if Dressen plays third."

Hank remained in right field, but Dressen had plenty of other miracles hidden beneath his baseball cap. He did build up a new wave of enthusiasm in the fans. The citizens of Milwaukee had lost those fresh blooms of undemanding enthusiasm that had marked the Braves first couple of seasons in their new home. Now, like fans everywhere else, they wanted a winner, or at the least an exciting pennant contender. Under Haney they had been an unexciting ball club to watch even when winning. Attendance had fallen to its lowest ebb in 1959. Dressen brought the crowds back to County Stadium.

He worked hit-and-run plays, he let his men steal

bases, he fired them full of confidence and made them holler with him from the bench. He even got them to argue with the umpires. He fired Milwaukee to its hottest baseball pitch since the team first moved there in 1953.

He did everything but win the pennant. He didn't even come close. The Braves finished second in 1960, seven games behind the Pittsburgh Pirates.

Even the weather seemed to conspire against the Braves that season. Milwaukee suffered a wet and cold spring, but the Braves suffered more. At one point they didn't get to play a complete game for twelve straight days. The hitters paid in their timing, but the pitchers paid even more dearly, for when they did get a chance to work, the damp cold stiffened their arms. Spahn missed his regular turn to pitch three times, throwing him off schedule and out of condition. Pizarro and Willey came up with sore arms attributed to the weather, and the Braves' second line of hurlers never got a chance to work at all.

Still, as Dressen hastened to point out afterward, the Braves' record would have been good enough to win the 1959 pennant without the playoff. They won eighty-eight games, two more than did the Dodgers in 1959, not counting their two playoff victories.

Actually, therefore, Milwaukee's troubles in 1960 came mostly from the Pirates, who surprised everybody in the league by winning ninety-five games. The Braves just couldn't overcome Pittsburgh's inspired dash to the pennant.

180

Significantly, there was no talk afterward about complacency or choking up under pressure. The Braves were obviosuly a rejuvenated bunch, in spirit and actual play, and they gave Dressen full credit for the change. He broke up the feuding cliques, brought back to the clubhouse some of the fun that had existed there under "Jolly Cholly" Grimm. He made them play hustling baseball and made them love it. They were a friendly, fun-loving team in the clubhouse, but on the field they displayed the aggressiveness characterizing any team playing under Charlie Dressen.

It wasn't easy to find fault with Dressen's handling of the 1960 Braves. If he hadn't promised so much, in his typically flamboyant style, there would have been nothing to fault at all. As it was, some of the sports writers needled him, but even they recognized that his style had paid some dividends.

For example, back in the clean-up spot, Hank led the league in the most important department, runs batted in, with 126. He also walloped 40 homers, just one less than league leader Ernie Banks of the Cubs. His average fell off to .292, lowest since his rookie year, but a bad spring start—the cold weather again—was blamed for it.

Hank wasn't the only player who profited from Dressen's line-up change. Adcock, under Haney two-platooned with Torre at first base, pleaded with the new manager for a chance to play regularly. "Play me and you won't regret it," he said. Dressen played him, and Adcock had his best year.

181

Catcher Crandall, long known as a smart catcher who couldn't hit, suddenly found himself switched from the bottom half of the batting order to second. "With that kind of confidence shown me I just had to make good," Crandall said, and he too had his best year at the plate.

That winter Hank was asked if he would take some time from his off-season job to help instruct some youngsters in the art of hitting. His initial reaction of reluctance was due to modesty. "I don't know how to teach anything about hitting. I just get up there and swing, that's all."

"But Hank," was the persuasive reply, "you're the best hitter in the league. You must have something to tell these kids, youngsters just like yourself when you were just dreaming about playing baseball."

Hank understood. He recalled, in a flash of his mind, the days in Mobile when baseball was all he dreamed about and worked for. He remembered Hartwell Field and the first time he saw Jackie Robinson play. He remembered the Clowns and Eau Claire and the jeers that turned to cheers when he broke the color line in Jacksonville. He had been very lucky. When he had played on the Mobile sandlots nobody had been around to talk to him about hitting or anything else concerning baseball. Nobody had cared much. How fine it would have been, what a thrill it would have been to have had a major league ballplayer come around and give him and the other kids on the Mobile Bears a few pointers.

182

"I'll be glad to come and talk," he said. "I don't know what I can say, but I'll come down."

He found, to his own great surprise, that he had more information to impart than he had thought. Especially when the youngsters began bombarding him with questions. He had come to the youth center with little more on the edge of his tongue than his old laconic reply to the question of what he looked for when he came to bat: "The baseball." But when he began to talk, the rapt hero-worship glowing on the young faces took hold of him. He felt himself caught up in their own unspoiled enthusiasm, and he told more about his philosophy of hitting than he ever had before.

"I bet you think big leaguers take batting practice just to loosen up their muscles," he said. He waited for their heads to nod that he was right, then went on. "I thought the same thing when I was your age. But there's more to it than that. Any time you take batting practice, use the time to work on any weakness you think you may have. That's what I do. I tell the pitcher to mix 'em up, fast balls and curves, all speeds. Players who ask for nothing but fast balls down the middle in batting practice don't last long in the big leagues. Come game time and they're breaking their backs on curves, sliders and change-ups."

"How about batting stance?" a youngster asked him. "Is there a good rule to follow about that?"

"If there is one, it's to choose a batting stance that makes you feel comfortable. If you're not comfortable

183

you're not going to hit. Me—I stand straightaway, away from the plate a little, with my back foot planted on the back chalk line. That way I can protect the outside of the plate."

"Did you always bat in a crouch?"

"Yes. As a matter of fact when I played with the Clowns I crouched even more. I straightened up a bit when I came to the Braves. I like to crouch, though, because pitchers try to keep the ball low and away from me, and from a crouch I can judge the ball-and-strike zone better. Also, I'm in a better position to swing at some of the doubtful low ones. When I have two strikes on me, you know, I prefer to hit away and get a piece of the ball rather than guess on the close pitches."

"Should every hitter learn to hit to the opposite field?" came the next question.

Hank smiled. "That problem probably has caused more friction between a player and a manager than any other. Naturally you get your most effective power when you pull the ball, that is, a right-hand hitter like me hitting the ball to left field. Some players it seems you just can't fool with on that, because all their skill seems to come with pulling the ball and teaching them to slice the ball ruins them altogether. But that's rare. Most players can hit to the opposite field sometime. I'm pretty good at it—they say, anyway—and I think it's a good thing. It keeps the outfielders honest, makes them play away from the foul line and more straightaway. Gives you more room to drop in the hits."

"But how do you learn to hit to the opposite field?"

"That's where practice comes in. When I was in the minor leagues Mickey Owen, the old Dodger catcher, taught me how to hit the outside pitch to right field. It took me a whole season to learn. Your coach will show you how to do it. He probably has already. Just practice. Practice everything. Practice will give you confidence, and that's very important. Remember, the pitcher still has to throw three strikes past you, no matter how good he is. You've only got to hit one past him. I figure that gives the batter the advantage."

Hank talked on and answered questions for more than an hour, and he returned several times that winter, discovering that he enjoyed the role of lecturer. Some people even asked him if he'd ever thought of coaching or managing. Hank shook his head vigorously. "What I want someday is a farm. Not just one of those twenty-five acre jobs, but a real big one like Spahn has, or Adcock."

Then spring of 1961 brought him back to the Braves' training camp, filled with new faces. Over the winter Dressen had lived up to his reputation as a doer by doing some radical trading. His first one—and most daring—was trading Bill Bruton and utility infielder Chuck Cottier to the Detroit Tigers for second baseman Frank Bolling. A proven fielder and solid hitter, he was expected to solve the problem at second base, Schoendienst's comeback try in 1960 having been unsatisfactory. To back up Bolling Dressen obtained fiery

Billy Martin from Cincinnati. The scrappy ex-Yankee was cut right in the mold Dressen loved best.

Pitching depth was another problem, but Dressen figured to solve it his own way, with what he had and could bring up from the farm teams. So he traded away Jay and Pizarro, a pair once very high on his list of esteemed youngsters. What he got in return was Roy McMillan, crack shortstop of the Cincinnati Redlegs, who would replace the 34-year-old Logan. The Braves now had the best infield in the league. That the radical changes would have any radical effect on the Braves' fortunes in 1961 appeared doubtful once the season was well under way.

Dauntless Charlie Dressen never wavered in his confidence, however. At least in Charlie Dressen. When everybody else had counted out the Braves he continued to repeat to all who would listen, "I can take the pennant yet. I can take it."

This led Cardinals' manager Solly Hemus to remark humorously, "If Dressen doesn't watch it he's liable to finish five games ahead of his team."

No matter where Dressen or the Braves would finish it was certain that as usual Hank would finish among the leaders in all hitting departments. No pitcher had yet found a weak spot in his batting attack, no effective way to stop him consistently except perhaps as one pitcher had remarked ruefully years earlier—by walking him, if you could.

As the great Rogers Hornsby said about him, "He'll

be murdering pitchers for a good many years to come before he winds up in the Hall of Fame. They'll never solve him because he's the greatest natural hitter I've ever seen. And I'll tell you something else. If anybody in the major leagues is gonna hit four hundred in the next ten years, it'll be Hank Aaron."

AARON, HENRY "HANK"

Born: February 5, 1934 at Mobile, Alabama   Throws and bats righthanded   Height: 6'   Weight: 176 pounds

Year	Club	League	Pos.	G.	AB.	R.	H.	2B.	3B.	HR.	RBI.	BA.	PO.	A.	E.	F.A.
1952	Eau Claire	North.	SS	87	345	79	116	19	4	9	61	.336	137	265	35	.920
1953	Jacksonville	Sally	2B	137	574	115	208	36	14	22	125	.362	330	310	36	.947
1954	Milwaukee	Nat.	OF	122	468	58	131	27	6	13	69	.280	223	5	7	.970
1955	Milwaukee	Nat.	OF-2B	153	602	105	189	37	9	27	106	.314	340	93	15	.967
1956	Milwaukee	Nat.	OF	153	609	106	200	34	14	26	92	.328	316	17	13	.962
1957	Milwaukee	Nat.	OF	151	615	118	198	27	6	44	132	.322	346	9	6	.983
1958	Milwaukee	Nat.	OF	153	601	109	196	34	4	30	95	.326	305	12	5	.984
1959	Milwaukee	Nat.	OF-3B	154	629	116	223	46	7	39	123	.355	263	22	5	.983
1960	Milwaukee	Nat.	OF-2B	153	590	102	172	20	11	40	126	.292	321	13	6	.982
Major League Totals				1039	4114	714	1309	225	57	219	743	.318	2114	171	57	.976

WORLD'S SERIES RECORD

Year	Club	League	Pos.	G.	AB.	R.	H.	2B.	3B.	HR.	RBI.	BA.	PO.	A.	E.	F.A.
1957	Milwaukee	Nat.	OF	7	28	5	11	0	1	3	7	.393	11	0	0	1.000
1958	Milwaukee	Nat.	OF	7	27	3	9	2	0	0	2	.333	14	0	0	1.000
World's Series Totals				14	55	8	20	2	1	3	9	.364	25	0	0	1.000

Index

189

About the Author

MILTON J. SHAPIRO was born in Brooklyn, New York, attended P. S. 115 and Boys High School there. At college (C.C.N.Y.) he majored in advertising and public relations and was editor of *Ticker,* the undergraduate newspaper. While a senior, he got a job as copy boy on a New York newspaper and six months later moved up to the Sports Department where he covered all the major sports, particularly baseball. He later became sports editor for The New York *Enquirer.* In his spare time he started writing sports biographies, and has become one of the most popular writers in that field. He and his family now live on Long Island and he commutes to his job in New York City where he is managing editor of a national gun magazine.